PERKINS+WILL

images
Publishing

Published in Australia in 2010 by
The Images Publishing Group Pty Ltd
ABN 89 059 734 431
6 Bastow Place, Mulgrave, Victoria 3170, Australia
Tel: +61 3 9561 5544 Fax: +61 3 9561 4860
books@imagespublishing.com
www.imagespublishing.com

National Library of Australia Cataloguing-in-Publication entry:

Title: Perkins+Will.
ISBN: 9781864703733 (hbk standard format edition)
                9781864704310 (hbk small format edition)
Notes: Includes bibliographical references and index.
Subjects: Perkins+Will.
                Architects—United States.
                Architecture—United States—History—20th century.
Dewey Number: 720.922

Edited by: Debbie Fry and Robyn Beaver

Designed by The Graphic Image Studio Pty Ltd, Mulgrave, Australia
www.tgis.com.au

Pre-publishing services by United Graphic Pte Ltd, Singapore

Printed on 150 gsm Quatro silk matt paper by Everbest Printing Co. Ltd.,
in Hong Kong/China

IMAGES has included on its website a page for special notices
in relation to this and our other publications.
Please visit www.imagespublishing.com.

Contents

CURRENT (continued)

ON THE BOARDS

st new hospital,  norial Hospital L (8) is

Perkins & Will celebrates its 25th anniversary and the firm grows its national presence with the opening of new offices.

Award: AIA National Merit Award to International Minerals and Chemical Corporation in Skokie, IL (10).

1960

rejoins the firm as the Director the Medical ssion, to ing a strong ctice. The firm rst high rise the Lutheran Minneapolis,

1963

Work begins on the firm's first international project, the National College of Agriculture in Chapingo, Mexico (11), and its first major high rise, the 19-story United States Gypsum Building (12).

First National Bank of Chicago Headquarters (13) is the tallest bank structure and the world's tallest skyscraper outside of New York at its completion.

1969

1971

Now with more than 600 employees, the firm reorganizes into architecture, interiors, engineering and construction management practices. Philip Will retires.

Award: Crow Island School is awarded the prestigious AIA 25-year Award, for a "design of enduring significance."

Lawrence Perkins and Todd Wheeler retire. Perkins & Will expands overseas with the opening of an office in Tehran.

1972–1973

1974

The Standard Oil Building in Chicago, IL (14) is the tallest building in Chicago, and the fourth tallest building in the world at its completion.

Amid a thriving corporate practice, the firm is commissioned to design 2 N. LaSalle, where the firm later relocates its office.

1979

1984

Award: AIA National Honor Award for 333 Wacker Drive in Chicago, IL (15) (with Kohn Pederson Fox Associates).

Perkins & Will celebrates its 50th anniversary; firm is acquired by Dar Al-Handasah.

1985

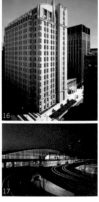

1988

Major projects include 100 North Riverside, Northwestern University's Research and Education Building (16), the International Terminal at O'Hare Airport in Chicago, IL (17), and Audubon Biotechnology Research Park.

Lawrence B. Perkins and Philip Will, Jr. (1) found Perkins & Will with first office at 333 N. Michigan Avenue, Chicago, IL.

1935

1936

Todd Wheeler becomes third partner.

Perkins, Wheeler & Will launch the firm with the design of more than 50 residences, many in the northern suburbs of Chicago.

1939

1938–1940

Perkins, Wheeler & Will team with the Saarinens to design Crow Island School in Winnetka, IL (2). Their collaboration establishes the firm's reputation as innovators in design.

Office closes for six weeks in 1942 while Lawrence Perkins and Philip Will, with Charles Eames, move to Birmingham, MI to help Eero Saarinen design housing for a WWII bomber plant. Schools, such as Rugen Elementary School (3) continue to be a growing market.

1941–1944

1947

Award: Perkins & Will receives its first Architectural Award, a Design Citation from Progressive Architecture for Indian Lake School in Barrington, IL.

Focus on educational buildings continues with Cornell University (4), the firm's first higher education client.

Award: AIA National Merit Award for Rugen Elementary School.

1949

1950

William Brubaker joins the firm now called The Perkins & Will Partnership; Barrington High School, in Barrington, IL (5) is its first high school project.

1953–1954

Keokuk High School in Keokuk, IA (6) marks the firm's first million-dollar building.

Awards: AIA National Merit Award for Keokuk High School (6); AIA National Honor Award for Norman High School in Norman, OK (7).

The firm's f
Rockford M
in Rockford
completed.

1955

1957

Todd Whee
from a pos
of Plannin
Center Cor
continue b
healthcare
completes
office buil
Brotherho
MN (9).

INTRODUCTION TIMELINE

Awards: AIA Architecture for Justice National Merit Awards for Fort Worth Police Station (29) and Dallas South Central Police Station (30).

2008

Awards: AIA/COTE, Top Ten Green Project Awards for Great River Energy (32) and Synergy at Dockside Green (33).

2008

2008

Award: AIA National Honor Award for Treasure Island Masterplan in San Francisco, CA (31).

There are currently 23 Perkins+Will offices across the globe due to strategic growth through acquisitions over the past decade.

With more LEED® accredited professionals than any design firm in North America, Perkins+Will is recognized as the preeminent sustainable design firm in the country.

The firm practices architecture, interiors, branded environments, planning + strategies, preservation + adaptive re-use, and urban design with clients in aviation + transit, corporate + commercial + civic, healthcare, higher education, K–12 education, science + technology, and sports + recreation markets.

PERKINS
+WILL

2010 marks Perkins+Will's 75th Anniversary and the distinction of being the first ever architecture firm to receive a National Building Museum Honor Award for Civic Innovation.

lonor
e for
cago,

Awards: AIA National Honor Awards for Desert View Elementary School in Sunland Park, NM (18), and Capital High School in Santa Fe, NM (19).

1989–1990

Award: AIA National Honor Award for 100 North Riverside in Chicago, IL (20).

1993

Award: AIA Institute Honor Award for Architecture for Troy High School in Troy, MI (21).

1994

1995–1997

Work begins on the International School, Beijing and MidState Medical Center, Meriden, CT.

Award: AIA Institute Honor Award for Architecture for Perry Community Education Village in Perry, OH (22).

1988–1999

Work begins on a significant mixed-use residential tower, Skybridge in Chicago, IL (23).

Award: AIA Firm of the Year.

Award: AIA Honor Award for Interior Design for Tribune Interactive in Chicago, IL (24).

2000–2002

2003

Major rebranding creates a new identity for the firm: Perkins+Will.

Award: AIA Honor Award for Skybridge in Chicago, IL (23).

2004

2004–2008

Haworth showroom designs across the globe (26) are characteristic of the strong, interdisciplinary relationships cultivated by the firm, culminating in One Haworth Headquarters in Holland, MI (27).

Award: AIA Institute Honor Award for Interiors for Haworth Chicago Showroom in Chicago, IL (25).

2005

Award: AIA Award for A Contempora IL (28).

Introduction
Reed Kroloff

When Larry Perkins and Philip Will opened the office that bears their names 75 years ago, they could not possibly have imagined the firm as it exists today: over 1500 employees in 23 offices on three continents. It's not that the partners didn't have ambition; today's Perkins+Will would not exist if its founders had not seen further than the practice they started on Chicago's Michigan Avenue. But at that time, few architects employed more than 10 people. You could count the offices with more than 100 staff on two hands, and most of the architects who practiced on more than one continent were war-wary Europeans in the process of moving to America. Imagining a global enterprise on the scale of today's Perkins+Will was simply unfathomable.

Perkins+Will is now one of the world's largest architectural practices. Through internal expansion, acquisitions, and mergers, the firm has experienced growth over the last 20 years that may be unprecedented in American architectural history. Further, that growth has taken place against a turbulent economic backdrop in the profession, with overall architectural employment gyrating wildly around boom and bust cycles. Through it all, Perkins+Will has continued its ascension more or less unscathed.

Perhaps even more remarkably, the larger Perkins+Will retains many of the defining characteristics of its younger, smaller self. For instance, the firm achieved its initial prominence with a groundbreaking education project, and it remains a significant force in that market sector. Winnetka, Illinois' Crow Island Elementary School, designed in conjunction with famed Cranbrook architects Eliel and Eero Saarinen, propelled the barely five-year-old firm (then Perkins, Wheeler & Will) to a position of prominence in 1940. The school was an immediate sensation in education and architecture circles, establishing a model for primary education architecture in the United States that would endure for decades. It was awarded the coveted "25 Year Award" by the American Institute of Architects (AIA) not long before Firmwide Design Principal Ralph Johnson joined Perkins+Will. Johnson has subsequently achieved some of his most important recognition—which includes nearly 30 regional and national AIA design awards—as the designer of a series of schools noted for their functional excellence and aesthetic distinction.

Johnson has worked with other building types as well of course, and the firm, under his design direction, has maintained its early reputation for producing thoughtful, unapologetically modern architecture. To be sure, there is a modesty to most Perkins+Will buildings; call it Midwestern reserve. But it is refreshing to look at the handsome Troy High School in suburban Detroit, and recognize both its patrimony at Crow Island, built some 50 years earlier, and its clear understanding of contemporary issues in education.

Clearly, no firm of this scale could limit its practice to one building type, and Perkins+Will specializes in markets other than education, including healthcare, research, workplace environments, civic buildings, and multi-unit housing. In Asia alone, recent projects include airports, corporate headquarters, medical centers, and entire new towns. This diversification in and of itself is not unique in today's global architectural economy: the ability to execute it with consistent care and attention to design is.

In a way, the birth of Modernism at the turn of the 20th century foretold the possibility of firms like Perkins+Will: multi-faceted international practices that would apply coherent design and delivery methodologies to a variety of architectural problems, each as part of the search for a better built environment. Architects would master the efficiencies of corporate structure in order to systematically improve the building process. To some degree, that has come to pass; unfortunately, often at the expense of quality. A bigger firm does not necessarily make a better firm. What makes a firm better, regardless of its size, is a passion for the work combined with the expertise to deliver it. Perkins+Will, as it has grown, has carefully acquired the expertise necessary to expand its markets while continually stressing design as the rallying force that drives successful product delivery. In short, the firm remains excited about its work, and it shows.

Consider the Interdisciplinary Science & Technology Building at Arizona State University. By the time Perkins+Will won this commission, it could claim dozens, if not hundreds, of university and research buildings in its portfolio. This one could easily (and profitably) have been executed as just one more, and very few people would have noticed (I know, I used to teach at ASU). But take a look at this building. It is a striking project,

with a muscular concrete frame and elegant louvers that bespeak both the precision of high technology and, in its careful response to the Arizona sun, a respect for the science of climate control (the building is LEED Gold Certified). The slight kick of its corner creates a thoughtful public space on a campus that has little of it. In short, the design moves well beyond expediency. Without adding to the budget or the program, it embraces material, symbolic, and civic agendas to become architecture. This is the work of people who look like they've never had the opportunity to build one of these before—and want to do more of them.

Which, one presumes, is exactly what will happen: Perkins+Will will do more buildings that are labs, and more that are offices, and more that are schools. And each time, they will approach them with excitement and rigor. How can I make this prediction? First, there is a long record here, and it is consistent. One has to presume that record is at least partly the result of leadership and a corporate culture that encourages achievement. Second, I recently served on the jury for Perkins+Will's first Design Biennale, which presented more than 100 projects completed over the last five years. The jury was unanimous in its recognition of the general (as well as specific) level of quality of the work; there were many very good projects on the table. This raises the third point: a significant portion of the work represented a new generation of designers. This was particularly exciting in its suggestion that despite the firm's global operations and multi-disciplinary structure, the core values and beliefs that have led it from a small Chicago office to a multi-national industry leader remain intact and are being transmitted.

That transmission will be vital as Perkins+Will moves forward. In a digital age, one where individual design and rendering methodologies have been replaced with universal software applications, there will be an inevitable "smoothing" of architectural differences. At the scale of a large corporate office, the result could be numbing in no time. The exciting work we saw in the Perkins+Will competition suggests strongly that the firm is not succumbing to this inertia. The next generation is fresh and confident. This essay, and indeed much of the attention of architects, is focused on the design heritage of any given firm, and that is important if architecture is to progress. But progress can be measured in many ways. In its remarkable growth and longevity, Perkins+Will offers a fascinating model of practice that should not go unexamined—one clearly built on a record of many, many satisfied clients.

When firms grow large through acquisitions and mergers, it can be difficult to create a cohesive culture. Perkins+Will, despite the fast pace of its growth, seems to have avoided that fate. At 75 years, the firm is large, and undoubtedly mature. But it is also vigorous and forward-looking. The work in this volume confirms that, both in terms of recently completed projects, and those still on the boards. Look at it all closely. I think you'll see the heritage of Crow Island and a promising vision of the future as well.

LEGACYPROJECTS

Terminal 5, O'Hare International Airport

Chicago, Illinois, USA

Design completion: 1989
Construction completion: 1993
Client: City of Chicago, Department of Aviation
Area: 1.1 million square feet

Described by the Chicago Tribune as O'Hare's "crown jewel," the 21-gate International Terminal 5 occupies a prominent position at the entrance to the airport. Designed to accommodate 100 percent of the airport's international arrivals and more than half of all international departures, Terminal 5 is organized around three primary levels: the upper level departure hall for enplaning functions including ticketing, security checkpoints, concessions, departure holdrooms, lounges, and airline offices; the lower level, which contains arrival functions including Customs and Border Patrol, meeter/greeter and waiting areas; and an intermediate apron level which contains the Automated Transit System (ATS) station and airline support services. A fourth level containing administrative and mechanical services is located on a mezzanine above the upper level.

The terminal has several points of access: an upper-level roadway for passenger drop-offs and pick-ups, a pedestrian bridge from the parking lot and the ATS providing access from domestic terminals and remote parking facilities.

The departure hall is flooded with natural light from an exposed structural steel truss system enclosed by expansive glazed sidewalls. From the hall, passengers enter the galleria that guides them to airline departure gates with its curvilinear roof. Retail stores and restaurant/concession facilities line the galleria, leading to the security checkpoints and concourses. Exterior views provide a continuous sense of orientation and numerous moving walkways facilitate passenger movement through the terminal.

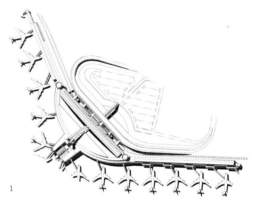

1

1   *Axonometric*

2   *View from tarmac*

3   *View of International terminal*

Terminal 5, O'Hare International Airport   13

Orland Park Village Center
Orland Park, Illinois, USA

Design completion: 1987
Construction completion: 1989
Client: Village of Orland Park
Area: 87,450 square feet

Orland Park's Village Center Complex, developed in response to the community's rapid growth, establishes a new image for this progressive southwestern Chicago suburb. Distinctively detailed with façades of banded masonry and clear glass, the complex occupies 12 acres of a planned 90-acre development.

The complex includes a village hall with government offices and classrooms; a civic center accommodating banquets and exhibitions; a recreation facility housing a gymnasium and related sports and support areas; and an outdoor amphitheater overlooking a man-made lake. The three-story village hall, fronting a formal, rectilinear village green, is the focal point of the complex, and its symmetrical configuration emphasizes its importance. It is crowned with a spire-topped clock tower, a new point of reference for the village.

A semi-circular covered walkway, spanning the lake, joins the village hall with the other buildings in the complex. Design elements such as columned galleries, circular pavilions, and arcade-style walkways are repeated throughout the buildings, reinforcing the order and hierarchy of the site plan while expressing internal function.

1

1   Main entrance of village hall

2   Axonometric

3   North view of village hall

14

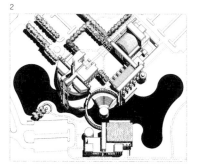

2

3

Peggy Notebaert Nature Center

Chicago, Illinois, USA

Design completion: 1995
Construction completion: 1999
Client: Chicago Academy of Sciences
Area: 73,000 square feet

The mission of the Chicago Academy of Sciences is to make the natural history of the Midwest accessible to all. This is evident both physically and metaphorically in the new museum's setting, form, and materials.

The angular masses housing the exhibits recall the shifting sand dunes that existed on the site before it was converted to parkland in the late 19th century. Their indeterminate quality expresses the dynamics of nature.

The building is embedded in the site and the roof hovers just below the tree line at its peak. By respecting the footprint of the park's maintenance sheds that formerly occupied the site, the existing trees and site contours were preserved. The museum's entry is through an incision in the landscape, emphasizing the building's integral and organic relationship with the site.

Beyond the lobby, a ravine with native planting physically and visually connects the museum to the pond. The glazed butterfly haven, featuring Midwest species, looks onto this space as well. At various points throughout the museum's exhibit space, exterior views connect what is outside to what is being explained inside.

On the second floor, a terrace connects to the bird walk that extends to the trees along the edge of the pond. The museum is an educational tool and a metaphor for the relationship between man and nature.

1

1 *Aerial view of museum from south*

2 *View from north of bird walk*

Opposite View from west

2

100 North Riverside

Chicago, Illinois, USA

Design completion: 1987
Construction completion: 1990
Client: Orix Ral Estate Equities
Area: 1.1 million square feet

The design for this 36-story high-rise allows varied program requirements to be expressed by separate components that solve functional problems. The air-rights site is over an operating railroad yard along the west side of the Chicago River, across from the downtown "Loop." The program consists of a leasable 23-story tower, a six-story data center for Illinois Bell Telephone (with higher floor-to-floor height requirements), a parking garage for 435 cars, and a street-level restaurant.

Developed in response to the clearance requirements of commuter rail lines crossing the site, the structural system uses steel trusses to support the suspended southwest corner of the building. The success of this system earned the Structural Engineers Association of Illinois' "Most Innovative" Design Award.

The building's massing is a series of vertically stacked, rectilinear blocks, each housing an individual function.

Spanning the site along the riverfront elevation, a 30-foot high covered promenade leads to the main entry. A two-story lobby is raised to the mezzanine level to allow the elevator pits to clear the railroad tracks below the building.

The 13-story base includes a six-floor, 250,000 square foot data center for Ameritech Services, and is cantilevered at the southwest corner from the exposed trusses above. From the south, these trusses recall the structure of the bridges across the river. Rising above the base, the office tower provides tenants with unobstructed views of the city and the north–south river corridor.

The focal point of the complex is a spire-topped clock tower, which accents the building's entry and, when illuminated at night, creates a radiant civic landmark in the Chicago skyline. Awarding the American Institute of Architect's National Honor Award to the building, the jury noted that the building "cleverly overcomes complex technical challenges and integrates itself magnificently within its riverfront site."

1

1 View from Chicago River

Opposite View from north

18

Crate & Barrel Corporate Headquarters
Northbrook, Illinois, USA

Design completion: 2000
Construction completion: 2004
Client: Crate & Barrel
Area: 96,000 square feet

For its new corporate headquarters, Crate & Barrel desired a classic modern design in keeping with the aesthetic of its houseware and furniture products. This new facility on a 24-acre partially wooded site north of Chicago includes office space and merchandising display space for sample products.

The building is essentially a linear bar with projecting office wings to one side. The building's siting and extensive use of glass and courtyards open the interior to the landscape and take advantage of the site's terrain and mature woods. A curved roof cantilevered from central columns celebrates the second-floor merchandising hall, the symbolic center of the company. The effect is a roof that floats above the masonry walls that enclose the office areas and extend out of the building volume to define courtyards. The large-scale curve forms a backdrop for the office wings, with cantilevered glass bays housing conference rooms.

1   Lobby

2   View from southwest

3   View from northeast

4   Level one plan

1

3

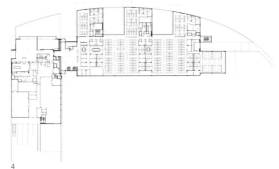

4

Tribune Interactive
Chicago, Illinois, USA

Design completion: 1999
Construction completion: 2001
Client: Chicago Tribune
Area: 85,000 square feet

The Chicago Tribune's abandoned reel and press levels in the lower levels of its landmark tower in Chicago provided 90,000 additional square feet of usable space for the company.

The first of the project's three distinct components is the new headquarters of Tribune's Internet division, a fully open work environment including 290 work sites organized over three levels. Several open and enclosed team rooms provide meeting space.

The second component is a two-level Fitness Center for the use of all Tribune Company employees. This 12,500 square foot facility provides a half-court basketball/multi-use court and workout and exercise areas. Men's and women's locker rooms each have their own sauna and 175 lockers. The fitness center also provides a lounge and juice bar area as well as its own towel laundry equipment.

The third component of the space is a new corporate conference center on two levels. Three new conference rooms accommodate 12 to 15 people. Two large multi-use training rooms can accommodate 16 to 20 people or combine for theater seating of up to 120. Each level has break-out and pantry facilities.

1

1   Entry

2   Meeting rooms

3   Plan

4   Overview

2

3

4

W.W. Grainger, Inc. Headquarters
Lake Forest, Illinois, USA

Design completion: 1994
Construction completion: 1997
Client: W.W. Grainger, Inc.
Area: 800,000 square feet

The goal for the project was simple: to create a phased headquarters facility based on principles of flexibility, connectivity, and responsiveness to the customer, the employees, and the community.

The first phase of the project was an 800,000 square foot structure made up of two elongated rectangular office wings linked by a fan-shaped central atrium. A 50-foot clear span structural system is based on possible planning modules and establishes an open column-free environment, freeing up the interior space to maximize flexibility.

The sunlit atrium is the heart of the complex, the area of connectivity within the campus, with bridges linking the separate building wings from both sides of the complex. All support facilities and amenities were located in close proximity to the atrium, including the food service area, a wellness and fitness center, visitor's center, and a conference/employee development center with a 500-seat auditorium. The atrium is designed to encourage interface, conversation, casual and formal meetings, and promote and elevate staff interaction.

Grainger's commitment to being responsive to the community set a standard for the campus structure that visually connects the building to the site. This was achieved by a strategy that conserves the 42 acres of woodlands and wetlands. Wanting to also establish a "good neighbor" policy, extensive berm and landscaping on the major frontage of the site spared any visual intrusion into the neighboring residential areas. The exterior of the building is clad in earth-toned hues of Venetian Gold granite and Villebois limestone that blends into the landscape's earthy hues.

The three- and four-story buildings were designed with a recessed base and top floor, thereby reducing the mass of the complex. Large projected eaves and linear projected screening elements above windows act as solar shading elements reducing the interior thermal load of the building. To further reduce energy consumption, all cooling requirements for the building are supplied by means of an internal ice storage system.

1

1 View of entry
2 Atrium
3 Site plan
4 View from east

Don Imus-WFAN Pediatric Center, Hackensack Medical Center

Hackensack, New Jersey, USA

Design completion: 1994
Construction completion: 1994
Client: Hackensack Medical Center
Area: 395,000 square feet

Don Imus-WFAN Pediatric Center was designed to create a colorful, humane environment for hundreds of children and their parents each year.

The master facilities plan completed for the medical center served as an effective roadmap for a series of modernization efforts within the 500-bed facility. Planning activities were comprehensive and included the establishment of a data base, an inventory of the existing buildings, and the creation of floor-by-floor plans for all of the medical center components.

After careful consideration of Hackensack Medical Center's strategic plan, a review of state and regional plans, and extensive staff interviews, a space program was developed to accommodate both projected growth and needed change. The optimal scheme identified three additions: a patient care pavilion, a children's ambulatory care center, and a surgical/trauma center.

The Don Imus-WFAN Pediatric Center for Tomorrows Children project was a direct result of this facilities master plan. It is the largest facility providing sophisticated outpatient cancer care for children in the eastern United States.

The 90,000 square foot, four-story building is divided into two distinct wings. Offices and meeting spaces are contained in the wing to the north of the atrium, while clinical spaces are housed in the wing closest to the hospital. Exam and treatment areas provide a new home for the children's cancer clinic and programs for pediatric behavioral medicine.

1

2

3

4

Temple Hoyne Buell Hall
Champaign, Illinois, USA

Design completion: 1990
Construction completion: 1995
Client: University of Illinois at Urbana-Champaign
Area: 109,000 square feet

University of Illinois' Temple Hoyne Buell Hall is a three-story building that houses design studios and faculty offices for the School of Architecture and departments of Landscape Architecture and Urban Planning.

The building is a working example of the craft of architecture, and a physical representation of the integration of landscape, urban planning, and architectural elements.

Four discrete elements are arranged around an internal public space. Two rectilinear loft-like spaces house the studio and department offices, and reflect the massing and façade organization of the adjacent architecture.

Linked with the hall's main atrium space is Plym Auditorium. The auditorium is conceived as a space in the landscape that is integrated with the geometry of the building, while maintaining its own integrity.

The other two spaces relate to a multi-level garden that is an internally focused, informally landscaped space. These are lyrical modern elements set against the masonry volumes of the loft elements.

1

1   Atrium view

2   View from south

3   Courtyard view

Temple Hoyne Buell Hall   29

International School of Beijing
Beijing, People's Republic of China

Design completion: 1997
Construction completion: 2001
Client: International School of Beijing
Area: 678,000 square meters

The design of the International School of Beijing is based primarily
on the planning and educational requirements of the International
Baccalaureate program. Similar to schools in the United States,
international schools utilize the "school within a school" planning
module with a high focus on schools as centers of the community.

The new campus comprises a 1,200-student elementary school; a
600-student middle school; and an 800-student high school. Facilities
for the cafeteria, media center, art, music, a performing arts center,
practical arts, home economics, physical education, and other similar
programs of the schools are housed in a shared facility. Approximately
100 housing units for faculty and staff are also located on the campus.

Through its modern interpretation of Chinese urban and residential
planning, the school itself is a learning tool for the local culture by
using the Chinese tradition of courtyards and processions to divide
the upper, lower and middle schools. The new facility is also designed
to support impromptu meetings with several smaller meeting spaces
throughout the facility. Each room also has the capacity to become
a full computer lab as technology increases. Interior drywall within
administrative offices allows further flexibility for future re-configuration.

1

2

1   Cafeteria

2   View from southeast

3   View of entry

3

Perry Community Educational Village
Perry, Ohio, USA

Design completion: 1990
Construction completion: 1995
Client: Perry Local School District
Area: 640,000 square feet

Perry Local School District's Community Education Village is composed of four elements: a school for kindergarten through grade four; a school for grades five through eight; a high school; and a physical education/community fitness center.

These facilities, designed in association with Burgess & Niple, are located on a 162-acre site distinguished by mature trees, ravines, and creeks.

Each school within the village is designed to accommodate 1,350 students and fits into a natural clearing. All classrooms enjoy scenic views of the surrounding woodlands. Three tributaries of Red Mill Creek have cut natural ravines on the site; one ravine serves to separate the lower from the upper grades. The lower and upper facilities are organized around formal courtyards, which are connected by an enclosed walkway that bridges the ravine.

1

1   Auditorium

Opposite   View looking west

Troy High School

Troy, Michigan, USA

Design completion: 1989
Construction completion: 1992
Client: Troy Public Schools
Area: 300,000 square feet

A wooded, hilly site in suburban Troy, Michigan is the location of this 2,100-student, four-year high school designed to accommodate the city's rapidly expanding student population.

The 300,000 square foot school is organized in academic, physical education, and art components located along a central circulation spine. The main entrance to the school is marked by a tower along a circular bus drive. Classroom wings overlook the natural woods of the surrounding grounds.

Special design/curriculum features of the school include a television studio, several computer labs distributed throughout the facility, a special education unit with a self-contained classroom and four resource rooms, a 750-seat theater, and a 3,000-seat stadium. The facility also features a fully integrated voice, video, and data system with an ITV distribution center.

When giving the school the American Institute of Architects National Honor Award, the jury noted that "... through superb siting, strong forms, and an engaging floor plan, the architects have created a focus on community activity, identity and pride."

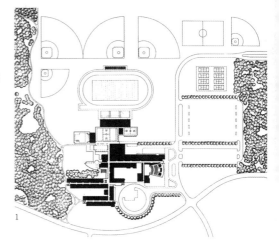

1

1 Site plan

2 Main entry

3 Entry lobby

4 Overall view from southeast

34

2

3

4

McDonnell Pediatric and Cancer Research Building
St. Louis, Missouri, USA

Design completion: 1997
Construction completion: 2001
Client: Washington University School of Medicine
Area: 227,000 square feet

Designed by Perkins+Will in association with Mackey Mitchell
Associates, the 227,000 square foot McDonnell Research Building
provides additional space for biomedical and cancer research programs.
The 11-story facility includes laboratories, support space, and offices.
A repetitive laboratory plan allows for maximum flexibility among diverse
tenants and future research practices. The construction was fast-tracked
in order to accommodate the earliest move-in date for researchers.

The laboratory facility is located in the midst of a dense medical school
campus, which includes the School of Medicine and four prominent
hospitals affiliated with the school. The new biomedical facility connects
to adjacent facilities providing direct circulation between researchers,
animal facilities, and clinical services located in St. Louis Children's
Hospital.

The unique floor plan also allows for a courtyard at the north side of the
building for pedestrian access and informal activities.

1

1   *Double height breakout room*

Opposite   View from southwest

Neuroscience Research Building

Los Angeles, California, USA

Design completion: 2001
Construction completion: 2005
Client: University of California, Los Angeles (UCLA)
Area: 130,000 square feet

The Neuroscience Center at the University of California Los Angeles (UCLA) acts as a key campus component linking the two Academic and Health Sciences campuses together. It includes generic wet laboratories to house neuroscience and genetic research, support space, vivariums, staff and research offices, as well as other instructional and public spaces.

A key design component was to promote interaction among researchers and encourage interdisciplinary research and a team approach. The design also allows for a series of building connections to adjacent laboratory and vivarium facilities, further enhancing the possibility of collaborative research.

The 130,000 square foot lab was initially identified on the Health Sciences Campus Redevelopment Study previously completed by Perkins+Will. The study resulted from an architectural and engineering review of UCLA's CHS after the 1994 Northridge earthquake. The review recommended the replacement of major portions of the campus complex as the most cost-effective way to ensure continued operations of the facilities in the event of a future large earthquake.

1   View from east

2   East side corridor

3   Site plan

4   View from south

1

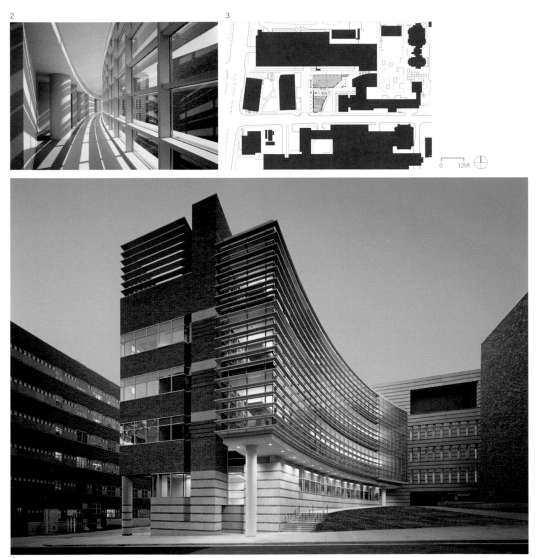

CURRENT PROJECTS

Brentwood Town Center Station

Burnaby, British Columbia, Canada

Design completion: 1999
Construction completion: 2002
Client: Rapid Transit Project Office
Area: 22,000 square feet

The Brentwood Town Center Station is the jewel on Vancouver's rapid transit Millennium Line. Because of its flagship location, it was vital that the Brentwood station be particularly unique, attractive, and enticing, to encourage transit use. The station provides a sleek, high-tech aesthetic for the new line. Hovering 30 feet above the Lougheed Highway, the main enclosure is a warm and appealing invitation to commuters below, and a safe, comfortable space for its patrons.

The station is composed in two distinct volumes: a streamlined platform above touches down lightly on a broad, low mezzanine below. The mezzanine acts as a public false ground, spanning the highway and creating an open and dynamic public space, while the platform enclosure above functions as a beacon, luring drivers away from the highway below. A single mass-produced glass panel, mounted on custom-designed rotating brackets, is used for the entire glazing system. This system is supported by curved steel and wood ribs of varying size and height, while extensive wood paneling in the station's canopy lends the project a distinct West Coast ambience.

The Brentwood Town Center Station has been recognized around the world and at home for its notable and sophisticated design. It is a dramatic and appealing landmark, and a striking addition to both the Millennium Line and the City of Burnaby.

1

2

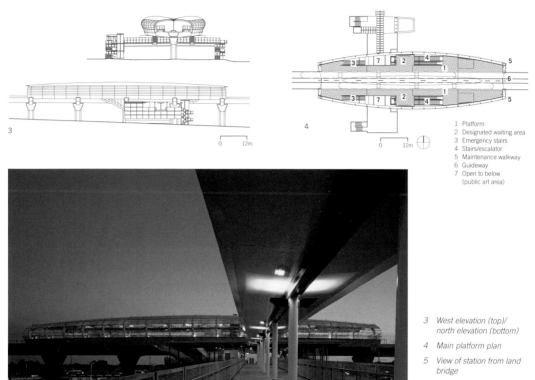

3

4

0   12m

0   12m

1   Platform
2   Designated waiting area
3   Emergency stairs
4   Stairs/escalator
5   Maintenance walkway
6   Guideway
7   Open to below
     (public art area)

5

3   West elevation (top)/
    north elevation (bottom)

4   Main platform plan

5   View of station from land
    bridge

6   Detail of composite steel
    structure

7   Main platform

8   View of station's connecting
    structural gutter

6

7

8

August Wilson Center for African American Culture

Pittsburgh, Pennsylvania, USA

Design completion: 2007
Construction completion: 2009
Client: August Wilson Center for African American Culture
Area: 64,500 square feet

Awarded through an invited design competition, this energetic urban infill building is a transformative first-voice cultural center that celebrates the past, present, and future contributions of African Americans to American culture, art, music, and theatre in the region and globally. The two-story facility includes a 486-seat proscenium theatre, 11,000 gross square feet of exhibition galleries, a flexible studio, a music café, and an education center. Named in honor of native son and world renowned playwright August Wilson, this forward-looking, one-of-a-kind hybrid institution engages the broad and complex diversity of this culture in Pittsburgh and beyond.

Strategically composed on a tight triangular site, the building exploits the moment where two city grids converge and the Cultural, Convention and Downtown Districts overlap to form a gateway intersection. The center celebrates the corner with a robust curvilinear form inspired by the full sails of the dhow, the majestic sailing ships that transported Swahili culture from East Africa. In a context of heavier, more opaque buildings, the curve breaks the norm and anchors the corner as urban art. The building is a composition of specific volumes and flexible public space. At both levels, flexible uses are organized behind the north facing glassy façade that extends 328 linear feet along Liberty Avenue. With optimum solar orientation, this transparency invites the surrounding historic context in to enrich the interior experience and engage the city. The building is a giant picture window framing the constant transformation, evolution, and influence of this culture.

To acknowledge the significance of the street as common space and as a stage for urban life, the sidewalk slides into the building connecting the street level uses. Open ceilings with linear baffles, ceiling rigging, graphic scrims and sealed concrete floors establish a functional theatrical aesthetic. The second level overlooks the street, and two large pivot doors subdivide the long space yet allow crowds to move fluidly between spaces during events. The highly controlled exhibition galleries absorb the triangular site geometry and are situated between William Penn and the sloped stone wall that is illuminated at night and glows with abundant indirect north light during the day. The formal stair moves against the stone wall and is the zipper between the galleries and flexible spaces that extend along Liberty Avenue, while the regal purple drum-shaped theater dowels the two floors together.

Opposite   View from northeast

2

3

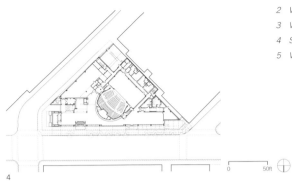

2   *View from east along William Penn*

3   *View from west along Liberty Avenue*

4   *Street level plan*

5   *View from second level*

0   50ft

4

5

Center for Urban Waters

Tacoma, Washington, USA

Design completion: 2009
Construction completion: 2010
Client: National Development Council
Area: 51,000 square feet

The Center for Urban Waters, envisioned by the City of Tacoma as a beacon on the water, is an icon seen from the downtown core, a living example of building- and site-sustainable strategies for future projects in the city. The three-story building functions as a water quality research facility for the City of Tacoma and the University of Washington Tacoma, receiving and analyzing water samples from the waterways of Tacoma and surrounding areas.

The building comprises laboratories, offices, conference rooms, a lunch room, an exhibit center, a customer service center at the lobby entrance, and related building services including a loading dock and mooring facility on the Thea Foss Waterway. A common thread among the design and sustainable solutions is that they each serve the end user. The users have participated from the start of this process, sharing aspirations for their workspace. The result is a bright, open, comfortable environment that fosters interaction between groups and strengthens connections between inside and out.

Sustainable strategies have been implemented in the design, including natural ventilation and sun-shading of the offices that serves all organizations. Offices are oriented to the west and south of the building to take advantage of views and waterfront air quality for natural ventilation. The lab areas, serving the City of Tacoma Science and Engineering Division and the University of Washington Tacoma, are located on the east side of the building with fixed windows due to the air filtration and temperature regulation requirements in these spaces. The labs were located on the site to buffer the noise and pollution from the street traffic to the east. Materials for the building's interior and exterior were selected based on quantity of recycled content, where the product is manufactured, the amount of VOCs (volatile organic compounds) in the product and whether the product is certified. Stormwater collection, water reuse, and responsible waste management before and during construction are also factors in achieving LEED Platinum certification.

Opposite   View from southwest

4

2

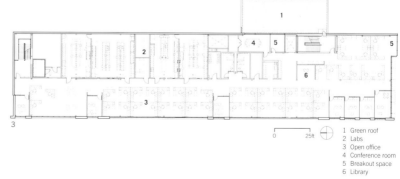

3

0   25ft

1 Green roof
2 Labs
3 Open office
4 Conference room
5 Breakout space
6 Library

5

6

7

Intrepid Sea, Air & Space Museum
New York, New York, USA

Design completion: 2008
Construction completion: 2008
Client: Intrepid Sea, Air & Space Museum
Area: 39,000 square feet (main hangar deck) plus museum campus application

The Intrepid Sea, Air & Space Museum is an iconic cultural institution and vital component of New York City's tourist and educational landscape. Located on Pier 86, the museum campus includes a visitor's center, the Cold War missile submarine USS *Growler* (SSG-577), a British Airways Concorde jet, and a collection of more than 20 historic military aircraft (including an A-12 Blackbird spy plane) displayed on the flight and hangar decks of the aircraft carrier, USS *Intrepid*.

The Perkins+Will Branded Environments and Architectural disciplines were "enlisted" to renovate the interior of the Intrepid's hangar deck (the primary exhibit space) including development of a new exhibit and display system standard to be implemented across the entire museum campus.

Working with the museum's curatorial department, the design team conducted a thorough assessment of existing artifacts, content, circulation, and audience types. It also analyzed educational, special events, and fundraising/donor programs. From this process, an experience strategy was crafted based on the juxtaposition of the technical "machine" aspects of the ship and artifacts, against the emotive human stories of the ship's crew, traditions, and historic eras.

The design solution established a new spatial organization that improved visitor flow and content comprehension, while a dynamic modular framework was utilized to support flexible artifact installation, improve lighting, enhance video projection, and integrate new interactive technologies. This experiential system's aesthetic was sympathetic to the ship's environment, while also respecting the National Historic Landmark status of the USS *Intrepid*.

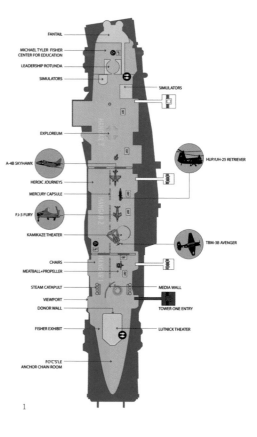

1

1 Artifact location plan
2 Kamikaze memorial
3 Looking through a "chapter portal"
4 Hardware exhibit introduction

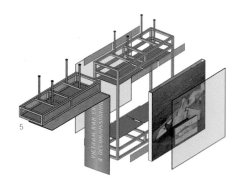

5

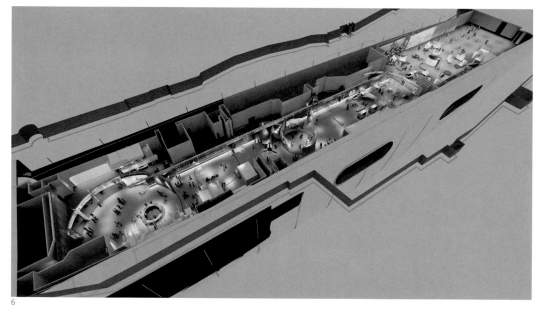

6

7

8

Los Angeles Police Department Rampart Station

Los Angeles, California, USA

Design completion: 2005
Construction completion: 2008
Client: City of Los Angeles
Area: 56,750 square feet

LAPD Rampart Police Station, completed in association with Roth + Sheppard Architects, is located just west of downtown Los Angeles and projects a proud new civic image for law enforcement. Design objectives included providing much-needed outdoor public green spaces for the dense, urban neighborhood, and providing a secure yet welcoming facility. The program includes a state-of-the-art police facility with community meeting spaces, a vehicle maintenance building, and a 230-car parking structure.

New structures are positioned near the center of the parcel to create public parkways for neighborhood use, buffer the secure facilities, and preserve a row of beautiful 60 year old shade trees. The composition, materials, and detailing palette (copper paneling, white burnished stucco, patterned ceramic tile, and concrete block) were abstracted from the community's abundant Streamline Moderne architecture, thus marrying the structure to its locale.

Innovative interior planning creates spaces that open and connect both vertically and horizontally, encouraging interaction between patrolmen and detectives, leading to better communication and crime prevention. Filled with natural light and connected to an exterior balcony, the fitness center's fresh air and stunning views of downtown LA offer a way for the officers to connect with the city that they protect and serve.

Working against the "bunker" mentality of 1960s-era police stations, public spaces are open and inviting glazed areas filled with natural light. Elsewhere, high glazing coupled with invisible security features provide requisite protection for civil servants within. The perimeter masonry walls secure the facility and provide an attractive backdrop to community activities in the parkway. At the south façade, a patterned block marches atop a precision block wall, forming an ornamental cornice that recreates the "ramparts" of lore while again alluding to local architectural traditions.

The Rampart station was the first project for the LAPD to achieve LEED Gold certification.

1

2

3

2 Conference room overlooking
  public green

3 Ground floor plan

4 Public lobby/front desk

Materials Testing Laboratory

Vancouver, British Columbia, Canada

Design completion: 1998
Construction completion: 1999
Client: City of Vancouver Engineering Services
Area: 4,284 square feet

The City of Vancouver's Asphalt Plant and Materials Handling Facility was relocated in 1999 to the north shore of the Fraser River. This new site accommodates aggregate handling and asphalt manufacturing activities, with a small building for the Materials Testing Laboratory. Although the project is small, it is an exciting prototype, demonstrating the economical use of recycled and reused materials in construction.

The highly rational layout of the two-story building accommodates laboratory facilities, with associated office and amenity spaces. The building's orientation provides unobstructed views from the second floor toward the river, allowing easy supervision of barges unloading at the site.

In order to achieve the 90 percent recycled content mandated, every aspect of the building was designed for simplicity and clarity. Exposed structural and mechanical systems inform occupants of the building systems at work. The design incorporates recycled and reused materials extensively throughout the building including: heavy timber structural members, roof trusses salvaged from existing warehouses on site, existing lab and mechanical equipment, light fixtures, and furniture. Other sustainable building design concepts, such as natural ventilation and solar shading have also been utilized.

1

2

1   Structural base detail

2   Elevation detail

3   East elevation

1 Entry
2 Garage
3 Mix room
4 Aggregate room
5 Binder room

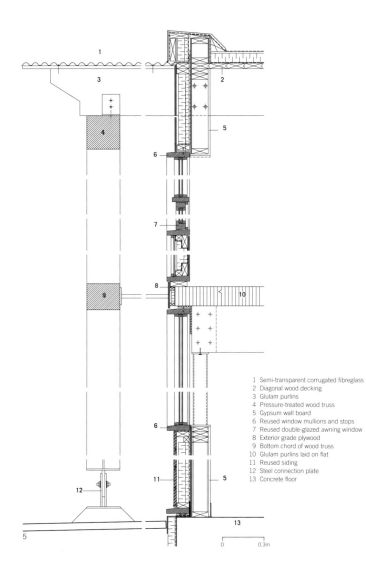

1 Semi-transparent corrugated fibreglass
2 Diagonal wood decking
3 Glulam purlins
4 Pressure-treated wood truss
5 Gypsum wall board
6 Reused window mullions and stops
7 Reused double-glazed awning window
8 Exterior grade plywood
9 Bottom chord of wood truss
10 Glulam purlins laid on flat
11 Reused siding
12 Steel connection plate
13 Concrete floor

6

Miami Beach City Hall Annex
Miami Beach, Florida, USA

Design completion: 2006
Construction completion: 2009
Client: City of Miami Beach
Area: 300,000 square feet

Inspired by its unique tropical location, the Miami Beach City Hall Annex manipulates light and shadow to mimic the flow of the beach's gentle tropical breeze.

This is accomplished by a surface of undulating metal blades that veils seven levels of parking and public services. The movement of the sun over the blades throughout the course of the day provides a sense of gentle motion. A continuously changing choreography of artificial lighting reflects off the blades at night. This same lyrical surface functions to provide shade and reflect daylight deep into the parking floor plates behind it. High-performance glazing, exterior sunshades, and a canopy colonnade allow for careful daylighting of the project's 35,000 square feet of offices that line the west façade.

The annex is situated at an important location along the north edge of Miami Beach's vibrant commercial district, creating a natural gateway from the larger scale of the Miami Beach Convention Center to the pedestrian culture of legendary South Beach. Local keystone accents on vertical elements and appropriate scale and orientation allow the building to create a dialogue with the existing, adjacent civic buildings. This contextual sensitivity is reinforced by the connection to the original City Hall, the design of a pedestrian plaza and park on the southwest corner of the site which, together with the building, form a complex that completes a civic center campus for the city.

1   View from southwest

1

Miami Beach City Hall Annex 67

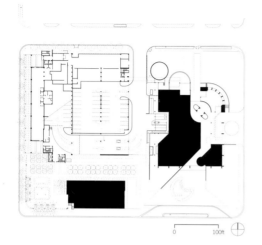

2

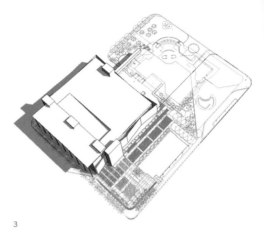

3

2 Campus site plan

3 City hall campus diagram

4 View from northwest

5 View from east connection
   to Miami Beach City Hall

4

5

Normand Maurice Building
Montreal, Quebec, Canada

Design completion: 2002
Construction completion: 2006
Client: Public Works and Government Services Canada / Department of National Defense
Area: 169,000 square feet

The Normand Maurice building is an office headquarters, warehouse, and armoury storage for the Department of National Defense (DND) and the Royal Canadian Mounted Police (RCMP), Canada Customs, and several other public bodies.

The lower portion of the building houses a drill hall, armoury, shooting range, fully enclosed trucking depot, and secure storage for the DND and RCMP. In order to fit this large volume into Montreal's historic St. Henri district, the extensive base is constructed of masonry and retains fragments of the original industrial foundry upon which the facility was built.

A three-story office bar sits above the warehouse and is shared by the RCMP and the DND on opposite ends. Three key architectural elements stitch this bar to the warehouse base. The first is a glazed corridor on the southwest façade that links high-security spaces and functions as a thermal buffer zone for the offices to the northwest. The corridor is clad with custom aluminum louvers. Behind the glazing is a thermal mass wall constructed from bricks salvaged from the original buildings on site. The second is a series of light scoops that spatially connect the separate floors, optimizing the natural daylighting and access to views. The light wells and south corridor act as ducts for the natural ventilation system and are part of the heat recovery strategy. The third element is an original building fragment that functions as the office main entry and interconnects secure and public areas of the building with the street outside.

The building was the first large-scale project in Quebec to incorporate the LEED requirements as part of a fixed-price bidding package. Sustainable strategies include a reduction of water needs by more than 25 percent through the collection of rainwater in an on-site cistern and the use of mechanical, electrical and other building systems synergies that reduce operating costs by 50 percent and reduce CO_2 emissions by approximately 800 tonnes per annum. The project has been certified LEED-NC Gold by the Canada Green Building Council.

1

1   Exterior view overlooking
    Montreal

2   Exterior elevation

2

3

4

5

6

7

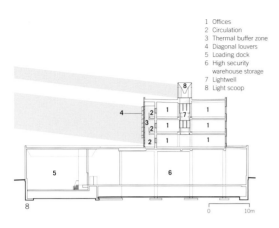

1 Offices
2 Circulation
3 Thermal buffer zone
4 Diagonal louvers
5 Loading dock
6 High security
   warehouse storage
7 Lightwell
8 Light scoop

8

0   10m

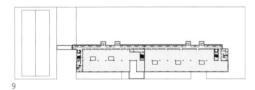

9

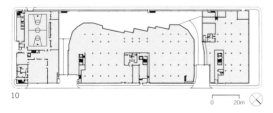

10

0   20m

3 Glazed roof and louver detail

4 Solar devices lining
   southwest façade

5 Detail of custom aluminum
   louvers lining corridor

6 Three-story glazed corridor

7 Common space interfacing
   with public realm

8 West façade featuring winter
   daylight control

9 Typical upper office floor plan

10 Ground floor plan

Richard E. Lindner Center
George & Helen Smith Athletics Museum
Cincinnati, Ohio, USA

Design completion: 2005
Construction completion: 2006
Client: University of Cincinnati
Area: 23,000 square feet

This building occupies a site on the university's campus between the basketball arena and the football and baseball stadiums. Located on the primary student and visitor circulation spine, this focal point of the campus houses all athletic department staff offices, student–athlete tutoring studios, ticket offices, booster club, and retail store functions. It is also utilized for both athletic and intramural locker facilities, training, and health services.

The Branded Environments discipline collaborated with the Richard E. Lindner Center's architects, Bernard Tschumi Architects and Glaserworks to create a unique educational facility. Responsible for developing the environmental graphics, archival display and electronic communication systems, the Branded Environments team designed a solution that expresses the heritage and bright future of the university's athletic and academic programs.

The project's goal is to communicate the combined benefits and notable achievements of the University of Cincinnati's educational excellence and rich athletic history, utilizing the building's central atrium space as a combined museum, archive, welcome center, and recruiting vehicle.

The design concept incorporates large-scale environmental graphics, signage elements, interactive kiosks, archival artifact displays, and new interactive/projection technologies to allow a variety of multimedia communications. These elements allow each sport and academic program to represent its particular history, as well as show real-time visuals of games or lectures in progress, highlight clips, and/or practice sessions within the facility to existing students and prospective student athletes recruited by the university.

1   *Celebration walk and trophy wall*

1

3

4

5

2 Four-story glass trophy wall

3 George Smith commemorative wall

4 HoloPro technology

5 Celebration walk, athletics

6 Experience map

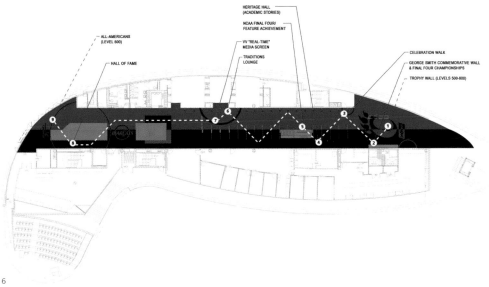

HERITAGE HALL
(ACADEMIC STORIES)

NCAA FINAL FOUR/
FEATURE ACHIEVEMENT

VV "REAL-TIME"
MEDIA SCREEN

TRADITIONS
LOUNGE

ALL-AMERICANS
(LEVEL 600)

HALL OF FAME

CELEBRATION WALK

GEORGE SMITH COMMEMORATIVE WALL
& FINAL FOUR CHAMPIONSHIPS

TROPHY WALL (LEVELS 500-800)

6

Haworth Showrooms
Various locations

Completion: 2004–2009
Client: Haworth, Inc.
Area: Various locations

The Perkins+Will Branded Environments team has partnered with Haworth to develop a comprehensive brand image, strategic positioning, marketing communications, and branded environmental language in support of the company's Adaptable Workspace, Designed Performance, and Global Perspective platform.

This work would demonstrate Haworth's evolution from a furniture systems manufacturer to a solutions-driven resource for "workspaces" made up of fully integrated interior architectural systems incorporating furniture, modular walls, raised flooring, ceiling elements, HVAC, lighting, sound, power, voice, and data technologies.

The Perkins+Will designs embodied Haworth's holistic environmental viewpoint. This philosophy was founded upon the belief that user satisfaction and productivity are directly related to individuals' control of their environment. This approach incorporated a broad interpretation of sustainable design (from social, environmental, and economic perspectives), providing the user with improved life quality, restorative space, resource preservation, waste elimination, and cost reduction. To support these tenets, Perkins+Will developed environments that incorporated elements such as reflecting pools, landscaped planting, and sand gardens.

This new brand and design platform was initially developed for the renovation of the Haworth corporate headquarters in Holland, Michigan. It was then adapted to meet regional design aesthetics and has been implemented across the global network of Haworth showroom facilities, which includes Chicago, Illinois; Santa Monica, California; San Francisco, California; Washington, DC; Dallas, Texas; New York, New York; Calgary, Alberta, Canada; Toronto, Ontario, Canada; and London, UK;

The Chicago, Santa Monica, Washington D.C., Dallas, New York and San Francisco projects are LEED Gold certified. All other US projects are pending Gold certification; international locations are designed to Gold certification standards, but are not eligible for LEED certification.

1   Chicago Showroom, 2004, "Jewel Box"

1

2

2 Calgary showroom, reception area

3 Chicago showroom, 2007,
   touchdown space

4 Calgary showroom, conference room

5 Dallas showroom, customer
   welcome center

6 Washington, D.C. showroom,
   product feature display

3

4

5

6

7

8

7 San Francisco showroom,
   reception

8 New York showroom,
   reception area

9 Santa Monica showroom,
   customer welcome center

9

INVISTA Inc., Antron®
DuPont Antron® Resource Center

Chicago, Illinois, USA

Completion: Annually for NeoCon trade show, 1991–2010 (Chicago)
Client: E.I. DuPont De Nemours & Company
Area: 3,000 square feet

The Antron® Resource Center is a year-round product exhibit,
conference center, and educational facility targeted to architects, interior
designers, and client end-users. It also functions as an office workspace
for Antron® product representatives.

The Perkins+Will Branded Environments discipline's approach was
driven by the understanding that the space must be capable of serving
the wide variety of functions conducted within the resource center,
while cost-effectively accommodating reconfiguration for annual
tradeshows and special events.

The solution utilized a dynamic architectural vocabulary that strategically
wrapped a three-dimensional, sustainable, and adaptable modular
framework around the perimeter of the space. This flexible infrastructure
incorporated display elements, audio-visual/data/power technologies,
lighting systems, environmental graphics/communications and storage
space. Adaptable wall planes were then placed within the interior of the
space to provide group, individual and "back of house" service spaces.

For more than 15 years, Branded Environments has annually
transformed the space to meet the ever-changing needs of the carpet
fiber market. The Resource Center continues to support the Antron
business as a three-dimensional marketing vehicle, while continuing
to hold the target audiences' attention. The space has continually
been recognized for design excellence, garnering more than 25 design
awards since opening in 1990.

1   Resource Center, 2003

1

2

3

4

5

Bank of America Corporate Center (Workplace Prototype)

Charlotte, North Carolina, USA

Design completion: 2006–2008 (multiple floors implementation)
Client: Bank of America
Area: 484,000 square feet (22,000 square feet per floor)

The Perkins+Will Branded Environments discipline worked in partnership with the Perkins+Will Planning + Strategy discipline and Charlotte office to develop a new workplace prototype for the Bank of America Charlotte, North Carolina headquarters tower. The overarching goals of the project were to reflect the unique brand identity of the Bank of America, to communicate its market position, and to provide an attractive, flexible, employee-focused work environment.

Utilizing a series of brand "visioning" sessions, the project team established the platform of "Journey to be the Most Admired Company." This theme embodied key firm goals and attributes including "terrific spaces," recruitment and retention, visionary thinking, and sustainability, which would serve to drive the master planning and prototype development process.

Bank of America's brand essence was fully integrated within the interior design, with feature areas that included the elevator lobby, a central circulation spine ("Main Street"), and a collaboration zone ("Associates Hub"). Elements of the brand were also woven into the fabric of the project's finishes, furniture standards, and signage systems. Addressing the financial industry's need for "instant information", the wayfinding system included the use of interactive messaging, digital information displays, and live data/news feeds throughout.

Reflecting the Bank of America's corporate mission, the project was also designed to achieve LEED-CI certification. The design solution incorporated access to views and daylight for all employees, as well as restorative spaces, wellness rooms, teaming nodes, and casual cafe space in strategic locations on each floor.

1

1   Main Street
2   Elevator lobby

2

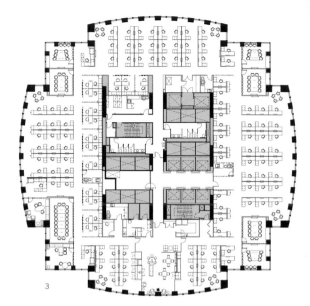

3

3   Prototypical floor plan layout

4   Diagram showing flexible,
    chassis-based planning

5   Associates Hub

6   Private office

7   Associates Hub

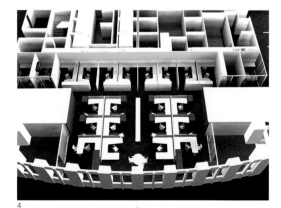

4

6

7

Chervon International Trading Company

Nanjing, People's Republic of China

Design completion: 2005
Construction completion: 2007
Client: Chervon Group
Area: 30,700 square meters

This project is a headquarters for a manufacturer of power tools whose products are exported to Europe and the United States. The client's business exemplifies the process of globalization, with global markets combining with local labor. The architecture symbolizes this intersection of global and local by reinventing the vernacular in a contemporary context to maintain the local identity.

The building is on an urban site, amid mixed development of residential, retail, and other commercial structures. It is ideally situated to take advantage of the existing service infrastructure while providing transportation options for employees. A pedestrian-friendly green buffer surrounds the building and helps diversify the streetscape.

The zig-zag contemplative path found in traditional Chinese gardens serves as the organizing device for the five departments of the headquarters. Countering this zig-zag geometry is an axial path that represents the more direct path of globalization. Two courtyards are formed by the zig-zag pattern of the departments: a public courtyard that opens onto the street defines the entry and a second courtyard is surrounded by employee functions and provides the choice for a more private meditative space.

The building mass steps to the south to allow light to penetrate into the courtyards. A sloping green roof unifies the massing of the five wings and also covers areas to form roof terraces for employees. A glass pavilion intersected by a vertical shaft of metal, which represents the client's product, acts as a lobby and entrance element. Water is used extensively as a visual and environmental element in the courtyards, as in traditional Chinese gardens. The sloping solid mass of the building and the water elements symbolize the tradition of the "mountain-water garden."

To protect environmental resources and enhance the interior environment, natural light is utilized to illuminate both occupied and circulation spaces throughout the building. Narrow vertical slot windows on the east and west façades provide light deep into the space and are shaded by protruding vertical screens on their southern edges. North and south façades are heavily glazed with movable sun screens and overhangs. On the exterior, the green roof and large planted areas reduce heat island effect and stormwater runoff, while the extensive use of water provides evaporative cooling.

1   Entrance courtyard from south

1

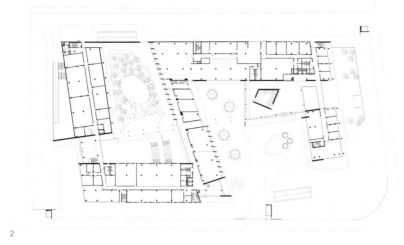

2

2   Level one plan
3   View from north
4   Lobby pavilion from south
5   Private courtyard from north
6   Middle wing from north
7   Client circulation tower

3

4

5

6

7

Confidential Financial Services Client

Boston, Massachusetts, USA

Design completion: 2006
Construction completion: 2006
Client: Confidential
Area: 13,000 square feet

The Enterprise Technology Architecture Group (ETAG) of this confidential client supports the firm's businesses in the delivery of its global financial services. The Perkins+Will Boston and New York offices collaborated on the design of the new ETAG work space. The Perkins+Will Branded Environments discipline was asked to craft a new client-facing strategy and branded environment to showcase this group's information management, service processes, and innovative technology solutions.

The Center for Applied Technology reflects the client's brand, strategic vision, and mission to deliver unrivaled financial services to its worldwide client base. The space is organized as a "neighborhood" of concentrated, collaborative zones providing flexible, adaptable, and updatable demonstrations. The design celebrates the client's capabilities and technologies via an information-rich environment that is as interactive as it is innovative.

Branded graphics supporting interaction and technology demonstrations provide a consistent visual language across the client's disparate organizational units. Integrated technologies connect the customer to real-time delivery models and provide a glimpse into future financial services, supporting new business development, client work sessions, and internal recruitment and training initiatives.

The centrally located Demonstration Showcase is an "incubator" of new ideas around which visitors circulate and interact. Clad in translucent resin, the thick curvilinear wall conceals a flexible infrastructure to accommodate changing technology, integrating messaging content, product displays, and lighting effects to create an integrated, brand-driven user experience.

This innovative facility was selected "Best New Briefing Center in the World" by the Association of Briefing Program Managers in its 2007 awards program.

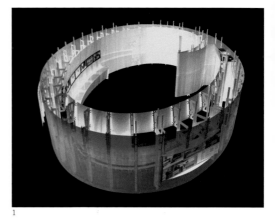

1

1   *Diagram of Demonstration Showcase
    showing flexible infrastructure*

2   *Demonstration Showcase*

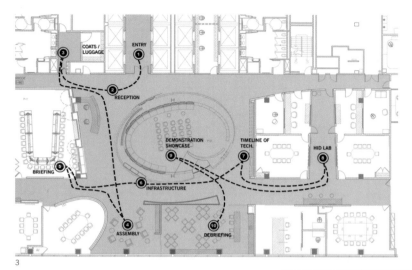

3

4

3 Customer experience
  mapping diagram

4 Visitor orientation area

5 Entry

5

Darden Restaurants Corporate Headquarters Building
Orlando, Florida, USA

Design completion: 2007
Construction completion: 2009
Client: Darden Restaurants
Area: 400,000 square feet, 60-acre campus

Darden's new corporate headquarters consolidates its brands and offices under one roof for the first time in four decades. In addition to providing the architectural and interior design for the new three-story, 400,000 square foot headquarters building, Perkins+Will provided landscape architecture services for the 60-acre campus.

The design is a glass-and-steel encased building with fewer enclosed offices for managers, more open space for cubicles and meeting rooms and several windows that let in natural light and offer sweeping views of the landscape.

The idea is to create a more open work environment that will encourage employees from the company's half-dozen restaurant brands to collaborate with one another. The facility houses office and meeting spaces, a 25,000 square foot corporate training facility and state-of the art test kitchens.

The project is LEED Gold certified.

1

2

1 Reception

2 Main Street

3 View of office wings
   across the lake

4 View of courtyard

5 Culinary stair

Equal Employment Opportunity Commission (EEOC)

Washington, DC, USA

Design completion: 2008
Construction completion: 2008
Client: Equal Employment Opportunity Commission (EEOC)
Area: 167,000 square feet

The mission of the EEOC is to eliminate discrimination from the workplace. Fairness, diversity, and respect are key principles of the organization's cultural values. For its new offices, the EEOC desired a design that strikes a balance between the serious nature of its mission and the exuberance of its culture. Another significant challenge facing the EEOC is the retention and attraction of employees. To achieve this goal, it is creating a flexible management structure, significantly increasing its technology infrastructure, allowing for alternative work schedules, and providing amenities for its staff. Based on the criteria developed at a visioning session, the EEOC and design team envisioned a space of bold statements that communicate the EEOC's goals of encouraging communication, teamwork, collaboration, and parity. Another key element of the space involved communicating the past, present, and future of the EEOC, which further reinforces critical importance of its mission.

The 50,000-square-foot floor places were a significant obstacle in achieving the goal of a collaborative and light-filled environment. The design team converted this apparent liability into an asset by placing the conference spaces and social functions at the center of the floor plate and infusing those spaces with kinetic forms, glass, light, and color. This "social core" was connected to the two building cores by curved, brilliantly illuminated red walls, which serve as a graphic canvas communicating the missions of the various groups within the EEOC, as well as creating a strong architectural wayfinding element. The conference and collaboration spaces are visually transparent and graphically interesting, featuring glass walls articulated with graphic elements screened onto the glass. This central social core of spaces is surrounded with "neighborhoods" of work and collaborative team spaces. Colors are primarily neutral, providing a backdrop for graphics and the fresh, airy feeling the EEOC desired.

The 15,000-square-foot conference center located on the first floor is used for all public hearings, training, and social events. The conference center has significant public use and is perfectly suited for the exhibit of the past, present, and future story of the EEOC.

1

2

1 Suite entrance from building

2 Fourth floor office suites, conference room and hallway detail

3 Large conference breakout space

3

4 *Typical administrative floor plan*

5 *Pantry*

4

5

Great River Energy Headquarters
Maple Grove, Minnesota, USA

Design completion: 2006
Construction completion: 2008
Client: Great River Energy
Area: 166,000 square feet

For its new headquarters office building, Great River Energy (GRE) asked the design team to demonstrate energy-efficient technologies that reduce fossil fuel electric generation and are transferable to its customers. The resulting design is a sustainable office environment that fosters GRE's collaborative culture while showcasing workplace productivity within the most electric energy-efficient building in the state.

Trails weave through the site connecting walkers, runners, and cyclists to retail, housing, City Hall, and the library. Metro buses stop at the adjacent transit center and GRE operates a fitness center with bicycle stalls and showers off the main lobby. Minimizing parking and maximizing green space further enhanced the transformation of this former gravel mine site.

Sustainable initiatives were introduced in the areas of water, lighting, air quality, materials choices, and renewable sources.

Initiatives to reduce water use include dual-flush toilets, low-flow faucets, and low-irrigation landscape. Rainwater is collected to flush toilets. Daylight harvesting led to a building organized along an east–west axis with 20-foot narrow daylight atriums sliced between 50-foot-wide office bars. Sunshades and light shelves are incorporated into the south façade and east–west façades are mostly solid to control glare. Daylight sensors trigger lights when daylight falls below requirements. Ninety-four percent of occupied spaces have exterior views and 86 percent are daylit.

Healthy air is ensured with low velocity under-floor displacement ventilation and a high-performance thermal enclosure coupled with lake geothermal heating and cooling. These measures provide 30 percent more fresh air in the breathing zone with 50 percent less energy.

Sustainable material choices include an innovative post-tensioned concrete structural frame, which uses 45 percent post-industrial recycled fly ash to reduce CO_2. Almost 90 percent of all wood is FSC-certified, 23 percent of materials are local, 18.5 percent are recycled and 96 percent of construction waste was diverted from the landfill.

An on-site wind turbine (which was also recycled) and roof-mounted photovoltaic panels provide 14 percent of the building's energy.

GRE achieved carbon reduction goals while demonstrating that green design is efficient, affordable, comfortable, and healthy.

2

Previous page
　　View looking southwest

2　Street view from south

3　Daylit atrium

4　Main lobby

3

4

International Media Company
Various locations

Design completion: 2007–2009
Client: Confidential
Area: 6,000–100,000 square feet

The design concepts for three disparate locations for this international media company combine a recognizable worldwide brand and distinct design standards with the particular qualities of the existing contexts in Beijing, China; Dublin, Ireland; and Queens, New York.

Perkins+Will distilled the essential and translatable elements of the company's brand: modern, clean design; daylight; branding through electronic signage and technology; transparency; visual connection; integration of art pieces; and a neutral palette punctuated with saturated accent color.

The new facilities are a manifestation of the company's mission and workstyle with distinctive fixtures, furnishing, and focal points. Each of the projects includes administrative spaces, broadcast studio space, conference rooms, and communal pantry space. The project in Queens, NY was unique in that the design included building a small jewel-like box of office space inside a 100,000 square foot data center. Aside from the data center in Queens, the projects range from 3,000 to 8,000 square feet.

In spite of the small scale of most of the projects, Perkins+Will has worked with the client to design the projects as LEED Gold, with or without registration and documentation.

1 Office "pavilion" in Queens, NY

2 "Lucky" red sculptural pantry elements in Beijing office

3 Stainless steel sculptural "clouds" in Beijing office

1

2

4

4 Open work areas in Dublin office

5 Pantry and central gathering space

6 Meeting/training areas

One Haworth Center

Holland, Michigan, USA

Design completion: 2006
Construction completion: 2008
Client: Haworth, Inc.
Area: 300,000 square feet

Haworth, a manufacturer of office furniture and interior components, commissioned Perkins+Will to design a prominent addition and major renovation of its Holland, Michigan headquarters. The aim for the renovation was to reflect the firm's culture, brand platform, and guiding principles by enhancing the staff work environment, showcasing product solutions, and maximizing sustainable design.

An integrated approach combining Perkins+Will's Architecture, Interiors, Branded Environments, and Planning + Strategy disciplines, resulted in a design solution featuring a new L-shaped atrium placed in front of the existing building structure. This north-facing three-story volume provides natural light and exterior landscape views for the staff. The atrium roof rises from the landscape toward the welcoming entry and features a plant-covered surface to reduce heat gain.

The office space is a reconfigurable "chassis" based on functional work types and is organized into "dynamic" (open office), "temporal" (rooms of movable partitions), and "place" (permanent infrastructure) zones.

The entire facility acts as a product demonstration lab for visitors, while also providing client engagement and mock-up areas. New staff amenities include training facilities, cafe, technology "genius bar," and outdoor terrace located in the bend of the "L".

An environmentally responsible approach leveraged a wide variety of deconstruction strategies and adaptive materials reuse techniques. More than 99 percent of construction waste was recycled, re-used, or otherwise diverted from landfills during deconstruction.

The project is registered with the U.S. Green Building Council for LEED-NC (New Construction) Gold certification.

1   Three-story atrium and Centers of Excellence

1

2

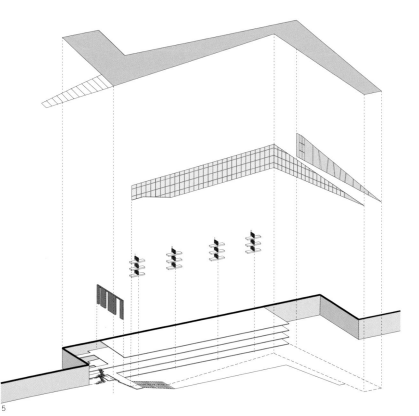

5

Research Triangle Park Office of Perkins+Will

Research Triangle Park, North Carolina, USA

Design completion: 2008
Construction completion: 2009
Client: Perkins+Will
Area: 9,120 square feet

This interior upfit is intended for 30 current staff with room for growth to 45. A key element of the design program was the need for collaboration spaces that were separate, nearby, and could accommodate groups ranging in size from two to fifty people. All workspaces have been created featuring the same size and character, from the office director to entry intern. There are no closed offices, but several shared closed rooms for telephone calls, private discussion, and conference calls were created. The shower was shared with the remainder of the floor's tenants in the interest of being a good neighbor.

In addition to being an example or metaphor of architecture, the space was designed as a technical laboratory for young staff. Ceilings and wall screens have been pulled apart into floating screens, strips, and clouds to reveal building infrastructure throughout the space.

The project is LEED Gold certified.

1 Gallery

Opposite Gallery stair to mezzanine

1

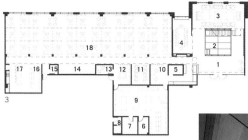

1 Entry/reception
2 Gallery
3 Lounge
4 Conference room
5 Storage
6 IT closet
7 Model room
8 Shower
9 Work room
10 Administration
11 Team area
12 Library
13 Huddle room
14 Pin-up
15 Phone booth
16 Materials library
17 Break room
18 Open office

3

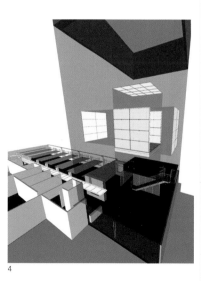

4

5

6

7

8

TELUS House

Vancouver, British Columbia, Canada

Design completion: Phase 1: 1998; Phase 2: 2003
Construction completion: Phase 1: 2001; Phase 2: 2007
Client: TELUS Corporation
Area: Phase 1: 130,000 square feet; Phase 2: 4,520 square feet

The aim of the TELUS House project was to satisfy a number of internal business needs while revitalizing an existing complex. The result is a powerful corporate presence for the company in downtown Vancouver.

The project consisted of two major phases: an extensive renovation of the former building into office and retail space and the creation of a feature atrium for team members that also serves as a seismic upgrade for the building.

The first phase included extensive interior and exterior renovations of office and equipment space. As an alternative to demolishing the existing nine-story tower, the building was recycled into offices, thereby saving landfill, energy, resources, and establishing the telecommunications company as a leader in environmental sustainability. The exterior revitalization was realized as an open, layered, and sophisticated new "skin" enveloping the old building shell. A double-glazed, fritted and frameless glazing system with operable windows is suspended from the existing building face, providing opportunities for a highly effective natural ventilation system. This second skin was the first double-wall/triple-skinned green building solution in Canada.

By not demolishing the existing building, 16,000 tonnes of landfill and 15,600 tonnes of greenhouse gas (GHG) emissions were saved. Yearly energy consumption has been reduced by 45–58 percent by using waste heat from an adjacent building, and efficient building systems operations will save an additional 39,000 tonnes of GHG emissions over a 75-year building lifespan. In recognition of its innovations in environmental performance, the TELUS House revitalization was one out of three projects selected to represent Canada at the Green Building Challenge in Maastricht, Netherlands.

The second phase of the project involved a new feature space and seismic upgrade. The TELUS House atrium was designed and constructed, utilizing a unique and elegant steel solution, which has resulted in increased structural integrity of the complex and substantially greater access to natural light for office users. The interior space also features two highly refined pedestrian bridges and a dramatic folded-plate steel stairway.

1   *Exterior view of atrium*

1

Building D | Building C (Phase 2) | Buildings A-B (Phase 1)

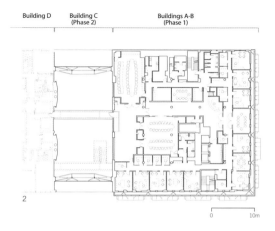

2

0   10m

2   Executive floor plan

3   Double skin façade protects existing building

4   Coffee bar

5   Atrium lounge

6   Cladding structural detail

7   Stair detail

8   Sky bridge

3

6

7

8

The Watermark

Charlotte, North Carolina, USA

Design completion: 2006
Construction completion: 2007
Client: Tuscan Development
Area: 30,000 square feet

The modernist steel-and glass-framed Watermark building is an owner-occupied, speculative office project. To maximize the use of its small urban site, the four-story building is set over the parking level. Due to the inclined site, the main entrance is at grade. Three sides of the building are clad with floor-to-ceiling glass to allow maximum daylight to penetrate throughout the building and to allow unobstructed views toward a new urban greenway and downtown Charlotte.

Small openings and stucco panels of varying shades are used on the west side to protect from the western sun and to create a scale more appropriate to the residential and small business neighborhood. The south- and east-facing glass is protected using inexpensive aluminum bar grating sunshades. The interior is designed to allow the structure to be exposed, and was painted to avoid the need for drop ceilings in the tenant areas.

1   View to west and south building elevations

1

2

3

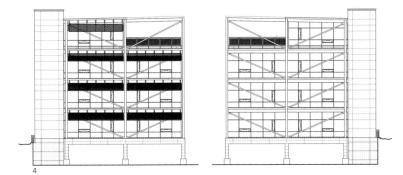

4

5

2 View to east and north building elevations

3 Stucco panels and exposed steel frame at northeast corner

4 South and north building elevations

5 Typical office

6 Reception lobby

7 Tenant floor plan

6

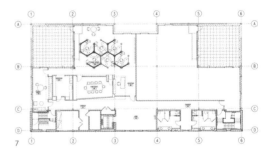

7

Mayo Clinic Replacement Hospital

Jacksonville, Florida, USA

Design completion: 2007
Construction completion: 2008
Client: Mayo Clinic
Area: 850,000 square feet

The new Mayo Clinic Hospital completes a fully integrated clinical medical campus with full inpatient and outpatient hospital services. With features and materials that convey ability, strength, and careful thought, the design projects the quiet confidence of the Mayo's legacy as a premier healthcare institution.

The Mayo Replacement Hospital is located on the same site as Mayo Clinic's outpatient, research, and educational facilities, making it convenient for patients, their families and visitors, and the Mayo Clinic staff. It is a rare example of a fully integrated medical center where comprehensive services and facilities provide specialty care for a full spectrum of illnesses, unite basic and clinical research, and offer educational opportunities for healthcare professionals and the community, all "under one roof."

The hospital has 214 beds in a six-floor tower connected to the existing Mayo Building. The tower is structurally designed for a 16-story vertical expansion. The main entrance to the hospital features an uplifting, inspirational canopy and reflecting pool. The canopy is carefully designed to be appropriate in scale for the current six-story tower through the full vertical build out. The corridors in the bed tower are 10 feet wide, providing suitable space for the resident physicians making rounds as well as the equipment required in an acute-care hospital.

The majority of the patient rooms are private and include a large window seating area and sofa bed for visitors. The large patient room design provides flexibility for equipment or services to be brought to the bedside as the patient's condition warrants.

The new surgical suite contains 16 oversized operating rooms for inpatient procedures, built around a sterile core through which the staff receives instruments and supplies. The six existing operating rooms in the Mayo Building continue to be used, making a total of 22 operating rooms.

The intensive care/critical care unit includes approximately 30 patient rooms, with the flexibility to decrease or increase in number as patient needs require. Mayo's growing transplant programs, which include bone marrow, liver, pancreas, kidney, heart, and lung, are located in the hospital.

1   View at patient tower and emergency entrance

1

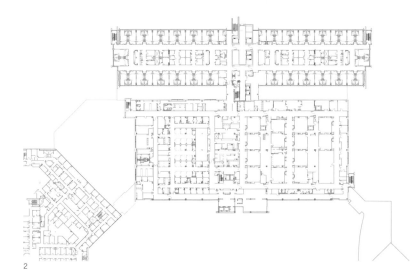

2   Floor plan with surgical suite
    and ICU

3   View of bed tower

4   Loggia at main entry

5   Nurse station view of family
    and visitor waiting on patient
    floors

6   Information and patient
    registration located at main
    lobby entry

2

3

4

5

Nancy N. and J.C. Lewis Cancer and Research Pavilion

Savannah, Georgia, USA

Design completion: 2005
Construction completion: 2006
Client: St. Joseph's/Candler
Area: 50,000 square feet

Set on a mature wooded site within the city of Savannah, this modern cancer care pavilion acts both as a dramatic backdrop and as a visual link to a series of reflective gardens, reinforcing the metaphor of healing within the garden. The placement of the pavilion preserves an existing grove of century-old oaks, which buffer the pavilion from adjacent neighborhoods to the north and west, while opening the pavilion toward the city's more dense development to the southeast. In doing so the design preserves virtually all of the site's existing foliage and utilizes most of an existing parking lot's mature oaks which, in turn, provide shade for the new, smaller flowering trees and landscaping. The existing stormwater depressions across the site are enhanced to create sculptured "rain garden" landforms with a variety of plants.

The cancer pavilion comprises two wings, one devoted to clinical and treatment and the other for research and administration. A transparent two-story lobby joins the two wings of the pavilion and opens to the south to a small grove of shade trees that frame a therapeutic labyrinth garden. Ample glazing accents the design's exterior and allows natural light to flow into the building. The glazed circulation along the north exterior wall reinforces the image of a healing environment by visually linking the interior lobby waiting and treatment areas to the series of exterior landscaped gardens.

The design transforms the east face of the building into a butterfly garden pavilion. A portico, reminiscent of the columned porches found throughout Savannah, defines an arc-shaped terrace and butterfly garden. The portico supports a trellis wing that mimics the shape of the garden below while shading the east-facing glazing. Embossed in frit on the glass wall is the original urban plan of Savannah. The pattern becomes a leitmotif that recurs repeatedly throughout both the pavilion's exterior and interior elevations as homage to Savannah's garden squares.

2

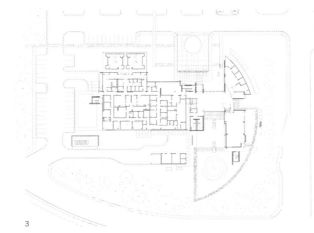

3

4

5

6

Nancy N. and J.C. Lewis Cancer and Research Pavilion   139

Peter O. Kohler Pavilion

Portland, Oregon, USA

Design completion: 2004
Construction completion: 2006
Client: Oregon Health & Science University
Area: 335,000 square feet

The spectacular site of the Peter O. Kohler Pavilion overlooks the city of Portland and the Willamette River. Part of a growth strategy to expand the patient care capacity of an existing hospital, the building acts as a hub linking patient care areas, teaching facilities, and the research and development zones of the existing campus. It also connects to planned research and clinical development both atop the hill and at the riverfront via a public aerial tramway.

The building is a transportation hub facilitating bus, pedestrian, aerial tram, and bikeway circulation routes to and through the campus. With entry points on the third, seventh, and ninth floors, it reconciles a 75-foot drop from one side of the site to the other and extends a unique, publicly accessible circulation spine (the ninth-floor "pedestrian superhighway"), creating access to new public spaces and gardens that serve patients and the public. Opportunities are maximized to create appropriately scaled outdoor spaces ranging from large park areas to public viewing overlooks, as well as intimate healing gardens inside the building.

The project, completed in association with Petersen Kolberg & Associates, consists of 11 floors above a four-level, concealed 450-car parking structure and relocated Campus Drive. Floor levels of the new building align with the adjacent existing hospital floors, facilitating direct functional connections between the two buildings. The primary entry on the third floor leads directly to the new parking garage. A second entrance at ground level provides a high level of recognition for the facility and a "front door" leading up to the ambulatory clinics, Women's Center, and the south-facing public view terraces.

The patient tower has two distinct faces: one is brick-clad with punched window openings relating back to the historic original campus center to the north, while a steel-and-glass curtain wall looks to the city of Portland and views to the south. The building acts as a backdrop to views from downtown Portland and across the river and is a beacon for the university on the hillside skyline.

Green design features include eco-roofs and roof gardens using native drought tolerant plant material. The project served as a Green Guide for Health Care test project.

1

1 South façade viewed from campus below

Opposite Roof garden view terraces

140

The Clare at Water Tower

Chicago, Illinois, USA

Design completion: 2004
Construction completion: 2008
Client: Franciscan Sisters of Chicago Service Corporation
Area: 750,000 square feet

The Clare at Water Tower is a 54-story high rise Continuing Care Retirement Community (CCRC). The project is unusual in that the functional elements usually distributed in several separate buildings in a typical CCRC have been stacked vertically, resulting in a new model for this program type.

The program includes 271 independent living units on floors 21–52, 39 assisted living units on floors 13–15, and 45 skilled nursing units on floors 10–12. Floors 3–8 contain 175 off-street parking spaces for the use of residents and their guests. Amenity spaces include three dining facilities, preparation and catering kitchens, a health and fitness club with a swimming pool, roof gardens, common gathering places, and places for worship. The top occupied floor is a party room for the use of the residents, allowing all access to the coveted penthouse floor and the spectacular views of the city and Lake Michigan.

The lowest three floors of the project are leased to Loyola University Chicago for new classrooms as part of its School of Communication. The main building entry, parking entrance, and loading dock share the first floor with Loyola.

A significant challenge encountered early in the construction resulted in revisions to the foundation systems. The primary problems were unknown vacated caissons from previous buildings on the site, sub-grade obstructions, and the inability to install the design foundations due to variations in the bearing soils and degradation of caissons due to silt and water infiltration. Responses included additional caissons, grade beams, micropiles, and dewatering wells in order to keep the project moving forward with a minimum of additional cost to the owner.

Another significant challenge was the state's evolving assessment of which floors were of institutional use. Its occupancy review and imposition of new code criteria grew from three floors to the entire project. The design team achieved a positive outcome through educating the inspectors and negotiating with the relevant agencies on behalf of the owner.

The project has made a positive contribution to the immediate context. It has earned a place on the Chicago skyline, with a commanding presence that outweighs its modest footprint and budget.

Opposite   View from north

2

3

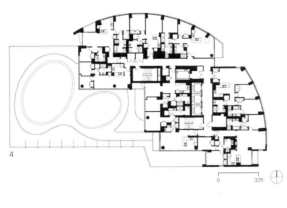

2 View from northwest
3 View from southwest
4 Typical floor plan
5 Base from northwest
6 Rooftop community garden

Arts & Social Sciences Complex
Burnaby, British Columbia, Canada

Design completion: Phase 1: 2005; Phase 2: 2006
Construction completion: Phase 1: 2007; Phase 2: 2008
Client: Simon Fraser University
Area: Phase 1: 83,205 square feet; Phase 2: 120,000 square feet

The Arts & Social Sciences Complex (ASSC) comprises two phases that represent the first elements in a new, multi-faculty precinct at Simon Fraser University (SFU). Phase 1 (Saywell Hall) creates a consolidated home for five existing faculties—the Schools of Archaeology, Criminology, Clinical Psychology, First Nations Studies, and the Centre for Forensics Research—and provides a link to the campus's existing academic quadrangle. Phase 2 (Blusson Hall) incorporates a new entry to the campus from the adjacent bus loop and houses the new Faculty of Health Sciences.

Saywell Hall and Blusson Hall are C-shaped buildings that bookend one another, forming a large, landscaped courtyard that fosters interaction. ASSC creates a strong public identity and a natural gateway into the campus by way of an east–west pedestrian concourse that runs the length of the complex. Areas of social interaction to nurture interconnectivity were of paramount importance in the design of the complex.

ASSC focuses on occupant comfort, which resulted in the provision of daylighting to interior spaces, including wet laboratories, which are traditionally closed environments. Program elements provide views to and from academic spaces as well as natural light penetration into all areas including laboratory space, allowing transparency and encouraging interest. Throughout the complex occupants are no more than a few feet from a view to the outdoors or the grand courtyard. The design also allows for natural ventilation wherever possible. Even spaces without operable windows due to safety reasons, such as the wet labs, enjoy visual connection to the courtyard through the north–south pedestrian concourse.

Above all, ASSC strove to recapture the vision of the original Erickson/ Massey design and update it with a reinterpretation of the same material palette and a sophisticated approach to green building strategies. The project features many of Massey's founding principles, such as the use of repetitive elements, concourses, and public promenades, and materials such as concrete, wood, and glass. The design also improves upon these principles where possible: repetitive vertical elements are updated as exterior sunshades that respond to the individual façade's solar orientation and the use of wood in public circulation and gathering areas is designed to be protected from deterioration due to weathering.

2

3

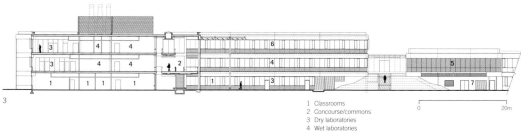

1 Classrooms
2 Concourse/commons
3 Dry laboratories
4 Wet laboratories
5 Lecture hall/theaters
6 Office
7 Circulation/mechanical/electrical

0   20m

4

6

5

Previous page
Internal courtyard

2   *Entrance to Blusson Hall*

3   *East/west building section*

4   *Extruded aluminum sunshades*
    protect interior concourse

5   *Student gathering space at*
    Blusson Hall

6   *Light filled, three-story atrium*

Computer Sciences Building
Toronto, Ontario, Canada

Design completion: 1998
Construction completion: 2001
Client: York University
Area: 104,400 square feet

York University is a 1970s-era campus that has grown to become one of Canada's largest universities, with more than 45,000 students. Responding to the pressure of a surge in enrollment in 1998, the University commissioned Busby Perkins+Will, in association with van Nostrand DiCastri Architects, to design a new computer science facility. The University requested a facility that was warm, open, and welcoming, flexible enough to accommodate unpredictable future technology, and as green as possible in its operations.

The building comprises laboratories, teaching spaces, faculty offices, and meeting rooms, arranged around a central five-story atrium. The atrium serves as a collector of excess heat from adjacent spaces in summer and provides a reservoir of heat for those same spaces in winter. It also is an important component of the natural lighting system, allowing daylight to penetrate deep into the building. In section, the building is organized in an ascending hierarchy of increasing privacy and security. The most widely used and publicly accessible undergraduate spaces are located at ground level with a direct relationship to the street and the most secure and restricted research laboratories are located at the top of the building.

The facility's design was based on realizing the potential of its infill site. The south elevation of the building enhances the university's ground-level circulation route, while snow, wind, and rain protection extend east and west to adjacent buildings. The facility opens up with a large glass elevation, a welcoming entry and open circulation space, and is organized around three functional components: a two-level lecture block located just inside the building; computer laboratories on the north façade, which capture efficiencies in energy consumption and communications systems; and faculty and research offices stacked in a flexible wing that parallels the main circulation space.

Toronto's cold-weather climate presented new challenges and the design response included several strategies. Nonetheless, the performance of the building in service, designed for 50 percent below ASHRAE/IESNA standard 90.1, exceeded predictions by approximately 15 percent.

1

2

1 Crush space
2 Lecture theater
3 Computer laboratory
4 West atrium
5 East atrium
6 Exterior deck

3

0   15m

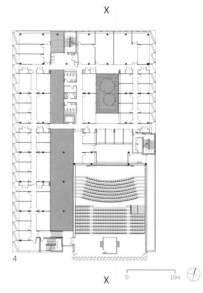

4

0   15m

5

3   Ground floor plan

4   Second floor plan

5   South view of entrance

6   South facing vestibule

7   Interconnected ventilation
    and day-lighting atrium

8   Spatial connecting corridor

9   Stack ventilation "solar"
    chimneys

6

7

8

9

Klaus Advanced Computing Building

Atlanta, Georgia, USA

Design completion: 2007
Construction completion: 2007
Client: Georgia Institute of Technology
Area: 210,000 square feet

The Klaus Building is a campus landmark. Located in a pivotal position, it creates the eastern entrance to the campus and is placed at an intersection of two major student pathways. The building demonstrates a strong image of modernity and contextual harmony, and has a welcoming presence.

The three-story atrium is a focal point for the science and engineering community and features a grand glass staircase and wall of windows that overlook the courtyard and the center of campus. An elevated pedestrian link passes through the center of the building, connecting it to other buildings, strengthening the academic community. The bridge's exterior laminated glass walls feature translucent binary code graphics with the name of the building.

The building also serves as a model of sustainability for the Georgia Tech campus. LEED Gold certified, the Klaus Building conserves natural resources and provides a healthy environment for all occupants. Over 50 percent of the site is preserved as green space. An on-site storm water filtration and collection system provides water for irrigation. Daylight harvesting, progressively dimmed lighting, energy efficient gearless elevators, and energy recovery systems contribute to a building that uses 40 percent less energy than allowed by current energy codes. Indoor light quality is enhanced with daylight penetrating deep into lab spaces.

Housing Georgia Tech's most advanced research labs for the College of Computing and Electrical Engineering, this building includes undergraduate learning spaces that serve a highly innovative, interdisciplinary curriculum for the College of Computing.

The interdisciplinary teaching/research environment provides cutting-edge facilities and technologies for robotics, supercomputing, information security, advanced digital design, computer architecture and operating systems. Specific program elements include: 70 laboratories, eight flexible computer class labs, five large classrooms with distance-learning capabilities, study lounges, faculty offices and a 200-seat auditorium. Informal lounge areas are carefully placed outside labs to foster casual interaction. A three-story parking deck beneath the facility holds 550 vehicles.

1

1 Site plan

2 View of east elevation with Atlanta skyline

3 Main entry at courtyard

Labovitz School of Business and Economics

Duluth, Minnesota, USA

Design completion: 2006
Construction completion: 2008
Client: University of Minnesota
Area: 66,909 square feet

The Labovitz School of Business and Economics marks another key addition in the evolving transformation of the University of Minnesota-Duluth.

The existing campus was organized around a series of connected classroom buildings that formed a chain along a north–south circulation axis. This dominating linear organization created a mega building that lacked clarity and identity for the various schools contained within it. In contrast, the Labovitz School of Business is oriented east–west, perpendicular to the existing campus development, creating an identity within the campus and a gateway for students approaching from the northwest. The building's serpentine geometry provides the requisite connection to the student circulation spine, which is essential during the harsh northern Minnesota winters.

The building is organized around a three-story, sky-lit common area surrounded by a two-level administrative block, a large 150-seat auditorium, and a two-level rotated instructional wing, containing classrooms for 40 and 60 students.

A rich palette of natural materials includes weathering steel, exposed concrete, multicolored patterned curtainwall, and a taconite feature wall. The materials serve as a reminder of the Duluth area's industrial history and as a device to further articulate the programmatic elements contained within the building. For example, the educational spaces are either framed by planes of weathering steel or wrapped entirely, as is the case with the major lecture hall. This iconic oval-shaped element, located adjacent to the main entrance, acts as an anchoring device for the free-flowing building that surrounds it. Above the classroom wing is a "flying carpet" of thin concrete plates that floats above the classroom wing and extends westward, creating a new front door and a literal gateway to the campus. Locating all the offices on a common floor of the building promotes a collegiate atmosphere and provides opportunities for informal interaction among the staff and students.

Another benefit of orienting the building with its long façades running north–south is its ability to harvest daylight and reduce the building's energy consumption while providing views to the surrounding wetlands and Lake Superior.

This building is LEED Gold certified.

156

1 View from west

1

2

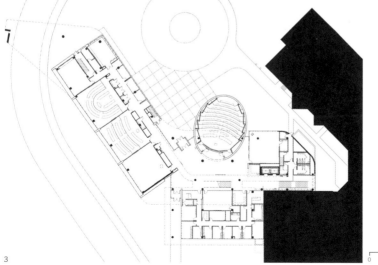

3

0　　32ft

4

5

6

Nicola Valley Institute of Technology

Merritt, British Columbia, Canada

Design completion: 1999
Construction completion: 2001
Client: Nicola Valley Institute of Technology and University College of the Cariboo
Area: 48,632 square feet

The Nicola Valley Institute of Technology is designed to reflect the cultural characteristics of aboriginal students and to provide the state-of-the-art learning spaces that promote traditional First Nations ways and foster student success. The building's program includes classrooms, faculty offices, social spaces, labs, a bookstore, a cafeteria, and a library. Functional spaces have been located to eliminate any sense of hierarchy within the building.

The design process involved intensive user group interaction and many site visits with native elders. The Institute's semicircular shape is the first gesture toward a circular master plan that was chosen because of the cultural significance of the circle. The building is oriented to the cardinal points, with the main entrance on the east axis to symbolize the start of the day.

The building emerges from its sloping site, evolving into a three-story structure at its center. The inner strip of the semicircular rooftop is planted, reinforcing the sense that the building has grown out of the landscape while minimizing disruption to the surrounding area. Traditional native structures in this area were mainly pit houses—dwellings dug into the earth and surrounded by a small ring of local tree species. This building is a combination of wood and concrete with a wood column structural system, visually representing pithouse poles rising up through the interior space.

The building is designed as a cold-climate green building, a commitment that is clearly in keeping with traditional aboriginal structures and values. A glazed ventilation stack with operable windows is central to this function, creating airflow patterns that ventilate the building naturally. Tensioned fabric is used in the ventilation stack for shading and is a reference to stretched skins in traditional aboriginal design.This technique is also used for the front entrance canopy. The exterior is clad with horizontal wood strip siding.

A challenging and successful scheme that adheres to the rigorous budget requirements of the Ministry of Education's value analysis process, this is the first phase of a much larger campus plan for the 43-acre site and will be followed by campus housing.

1   West elevation with adjustable sunshades and indigenous vegetation

1

2

3

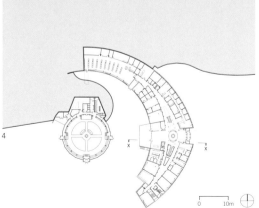

4

2   *South elevation*

3   *West elevation*

4   *Ground floor plan*

0   10m

6

7

North Campus Residence Hall

Bristol, Rhode Island, USA

Design completion: 2008
Construction completion: 2009
Client: Roger Williams University
Area: 120,000 square feet

This new 350-bed residence hall was designed to fulfill the university's wish to house a higher percentage of its students on campus while exploring options for future expansion. The site is in an undeveloped precinct on the edge of the campus, bordered by a large parking structure to the north, and playing fields and the academic core to the south.

The site is at a transition from the primary campus organizing grid to a different rotated grid in the north campus. The V-shaped building configuration facilitates this transition and creates an outdoor courtyard associated with the residence hall. In the plan for expansion, a larger residential quadrangle to be shared with future residence halls is proposed to the north. An important goal in the creation of these open spaces is to establish a sense of community at various scales—from the precinct, to the building, the floor, and finally, the individual suite.

Equally important is the routing of pedestrian paths through the new district and the location of building entrances along those paths. One major path, from the parking facility through the playing fields to the campus core, is channeled between the two wings of the new residence hall and the common space at the head of the V. The building frames a primary entrance to the campus from the north in dramatic fashion, with glass bridges containing lounges spanning the path and connecting the wings with the common space. A cafe, convenience store, and game room, all located at the ground level, serve both the residents and commuters en route between the parking structure and campus.

The material palette reinforces the concept of the building while responding to its context. The outer walls of the residence hall, facing the campus, are predominantly brick, continuing a campus standard. In the courtyard, a transition is made to a wood/phenolic panel. The wood creates a warm atmosphere and helps define the courtyard as an outdoor room for the students. The gateway formed by the building is clad entirely in bright gold panels, highly visible from a distance along the campus paths.

1   View from north portal

1

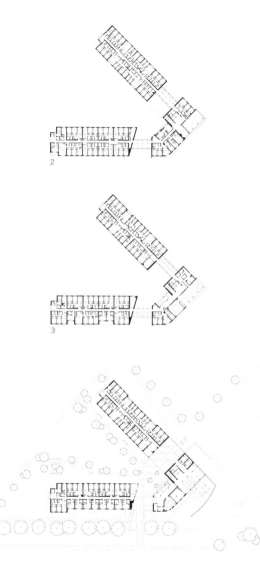

2

3

4

5

6

168

7

8

9

8   Courtyard elevation

9   Great room

10 Great room fireplace

NYU Stern School of Business Concourse Renovation Project

New York, New York, USA

Design completion: 2009
Construction completion: 2010
Client: New York University
Area: 90,000 square feet

NYU's Stern School of Business, located on a dense urban site at Washington Square Park on the edge of the Greenwich Village Historic District, retained Perkins+Will to renovate and connect all undergraduate instructional space in the two basement levels of its three buildings.

The design emphasizes connectedness and transparency by reconfiguring and reinventing the image the school presents to the city and broader business community.

The final design transforms the existing outdated rabbit-warren of vintage 1950s basement classrooms into a state-of-the-art instructional center. The new classrooms are linked to one another by inviting light-filled corridors, which are in turn punctuated by casual lounge and gathering spaces. These touch-down areas promote the interaction between students and faculty that make for a vibrant academic community. Branding, graphics and wayfinding by Perkins+Will Branded Environments group augment and enhance the experience of a world class educational facility.

The heart of the project is a central three-story atrium that carries light and energy from the plaza level to the concourses below. A central corridor under the plaza has also been filled with natural light by the introduction of a walkable skylight that penetrates down through the two levels. Designed with sustainability in mind, the NYU Stern Concourse renovation project is registered for LEED CI-Silver certification. The result has transformed some of the least desirable spaces in the NYU inventory into some of the most exciting and memorable.

Opposite   Atrium

3

2 Branding elements in atrium

3 Transparent entrance

4 Skylights

5 Skylights

4

5

Saint Cloud Technical College (SCTC) Workforce Center Addition & Renovation

St. Cloud, Minnesota, USA

Design completion: 2005
Construction completion: 2008
Client: Minnesota State Colleges & Universities System (MNSCU)
Area: 43,000 square feet (new); 44,000 square feet (renovation)

Saint Cloud Technical College (SCTC) is a two-year college founded in 1965 as part of the Minnesota State Colleges & Universities (MNSCU) system. Forty years of steady growth and incremental expansion have yielded a 300,000 square foot facility packed along windowless hallways with two dozen different exterior entry locations. With student demand pushing for more growth, college leadership sought a design vision that could redefine the long-term functional performance of the facility through strengthened campus identity and improved student wayfinding.

The first goal was to design 43,000 square feet of expansion space for the college that includes state-of-the-art "smart" classrooms, ITV classrooms, and science classrooms along with registration, admissions, financial services and business offices.

The second goal was to renovate 44,000 square feet into dividable lecture halls, media center, testing rooms, staff offices, and counseling rooms to serve as the new home for Minnesota Workforce Center. Collocating the college and workforce center will strengthen their collaborative partnership in training local residents.

The third goal was to uncover the college's unique identity within its community and improve student wayfinding with a new "front door", new interactive spaces, and a clear hierarchy of paths.

The resulting design is a two-story brick, glass, and copper-clad "main entry and main street" circulation spine that links expansion and renovation with parking and green space. This simple pathway is crafted from underutilized existing space, directly increasing overall building functionality and decreasing new construction. Orienting "main street" along the east–west axis allows daylight and views into the building while minimizing heat gain and glare at classrooms or labs. DOE II energy models were used to achieve energy reductions through increased building insulation, new high-performance windows, daylight sensors, and digital system controls. Water use was reduced through low-flow faucets and low irrigation landscape.

Through design, SCTC's monolithic building has been re-integrated within its site, suggesting the more porous boundaries typical of college campuses and the hope of expanding relationships between students, visitors, and neighbors.

1   View from north campus green
2   View of west campus courtyard

1

3

4

5

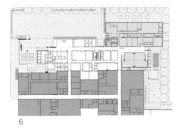

3　East courtyard
4　West porch
5　West porch
6　Main and upper level plans
7　East courtyard
8　Main entry

6

8

7

University of Washington School of Medicine Phase 2
Seattle, Washington, USA

Design completion: 2006
Construction completion: 2008
Client: University of Washington
Area: 441,640 square feet

The form of this school of medicine, featuring aluminum, glass, and metal, reveals its functionality and expresses a modern architecture that is a departure from other medical and scientific buildings in the region. From its inviting courtyard, nestled between the lab and administration buildings, to its landscaped connection between two main streets, the planning and design highlights integration with the community and neighborhood.

The master plan for Phase 2 drastically improves the School of Medicine's research capabilities. The open spaces foster collaboration and provide great views and ample sunlight while enhancing the quality of the indoor spaces. The unique lab flexibility allows the space to adapt to emerging technologies and research objectives. Common spaces, conferencing, and break areas on every floor are placed to encourage interaction and team building among scientists and technicians.

The exterior of the lab building is a visually stunning geometric vertical expression of transparent and translucent glass panels that establishes the vocabulary for the other façades, and is inspired by the proportions used from the adjacent 1960s Phase I building. The innovative but delicate stainless steel screens function as a sun shading device for the laboratories along the west and south façades. The screens reveal a play of light and perspective, adding to the intrigue and complexity of the curtain wall. The central core of the lab research building and the administration building is clad in white-painted aluminum panels and holds the glass and aluminum transparent lab and office enclosures above the ground. The central core contains all of the support and service spaces. At the ends, shared conference rooms are stacked vertically with wood louvers for sun shading.

The exterior design of the administration building has ties with the curtain wall of the research lab building, but includes programmatic elemental variations. The vertical geometric composition here is articulated around the slightly recessed operable awing windows, which admit fresh air into the building. These windows articulate the façades with a vertical rhythm while saving cooling costs. The integration of design and sustainability is an integral part of this plan.

1   Southwest corner

1

2

4

3

5

6

7

8

9

University of Washington School of Medicine Phase 2   183

Atrisco Heritage Academy

Albuquerque, New Mexico, USA

Design completion: 2007
Construction completion: 2010
Client: Albuquerque Public Schools
Area: 440,000 square feet

Located on the gently sloping southwest mesa above the Rio Grande
River Valley of Albuquerque, New Mexico, the Atrisco Heritage Academy
has become the cultural center of the southwest community. Designed
to initially serve 2,400 students with a capacity for 3,100 students,
the campus is comprised of 440,000 square feet of instructional spaces,
a media center/library, a performing arts complex and theatre, physical
education facilities, and a full complement of community use facilities.
Completed in association with FBT Architects, the campus provides
"Career Academies" comprised of small learning communities. The
integrated curriculum approach supports student-centered collaborative
learning within flexible and adaptable spaces.

*The National School Boards Association** recognized this new campus
as the grand prize recipient of its highest design honor in 2009, stating:
"the Jury felt the academy structure represents a best practice for new
high school design."

Three distinct goals were identified as design objectives for the site:
preserving the *past*; celebrating the cultural diversity of the *present*;
and embracing the *future*.

Preservation of the natural landscape edges and the outer ring of
community-use programmatic spaces shields the campus from seasonal
monsoons, prevailing winds, and dust storms, thereby preserving the
landscape of the mesa and its climate.

Inspired by the Rio Grande River, the exterior courtyard is based
on the movement of students flowing through the campus. It offers
opportunities for social interaction while celebrating the dramatic
setting of the site and the cultural diversity of the community.

The orientation of the academic buildings affords every classroom
unrestricted views over the Rio Grande River Valley and the vibrant
colors of the Sandia Mountains. This orientation also maximizes natural
light into primary academic spaces. The grouping and scale of the
buildings reads as a single "line" drawn within the desert landscape
symbolizing change.

1 *Academy/instructional space*

1

2 Floor plan
3 Community center/entry
4 Student courtyard
5 Media center
6 Academy commons
7 Student commons
8 Student collaboration spaces

3

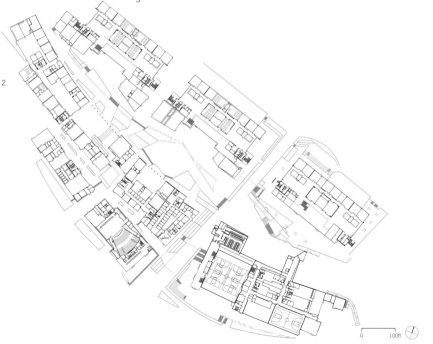

2

0   100ft

4

5

6

7

8

Blythewood High School

Columbia, South Carolina, USA

Design completion: 2002
Construction completion: 2005
Client: Richland School District Two
Area: 294,000 square feet

Blythewood High School is the fourth high school in Richland School District Two, a progressive, nationally recognized district in suburban Columbia, South Carolina. The high school facility was planned for 1,700 students with a core that supports 2,000 students.

Facility guidelines were created for the school through a collaborative, participatory process with the community. The guidelines placed emphasis on the school being a flexible, learner-centered facility designed to serve both students and the community.

The building is broadly organized into academic and arts/wellness areas, connected by a cluster of central community spaces. The academic areas contain classroom space for both core and specialty curriculum, including science and vocational technology labs. The core classrooms are clustered into four academic houses, each supported by its own grouping of satellite administration, resource, and breakout areas.

The central community spaces include the media center, commons/cafeteria, and cyber cafe; all are located at the heart of the school near the main lobby, making them easily accessible for daily student use as well as after-school, evening, or weekend events. The central administration, central health, and student activities center are also located here, enabling school administrators to efficiently supervise student activity and ensure safety.

Beyond the central community spaces are arts and wellness areas that include a 500-seat auditorium, music/art/drama classrooms, a 2,000-seat collegiate basketball gymnasium, auxiliary gym, locker rooms, and satellite administrative rooms.

Opposite   View from east

2 View from north

3 Entry from north

4 Level one plan

5 Agriculture education shop

6 Cyber cafe

4

0   64ft

5

6

Central Middle School

Columbus, Indiana, USA

Design completion: 2005
Construction completion: 2007
Client: Bartholomew Consolidated School Corporation
Area: 171,000 square feet

The new Central Middle School replaces a 100-year-old old school located on the same site in Columbus' architecturally significant downtown district. It creates new urban open space for Columbus, Indiana while providing a synergistic learning environment for 1,000 students in grades seven through eight. The north–south massing defines a public open space in conjunction with Gunnar Birkert's Lincoln Elementary School. This new greenway connects 5th and 7th Street and creates an educational park for Columbus.

The building was planned for flexibility and agility to easily accommodate future change. Two zones were created: an academic zone and a public zone. The L-shaped plan includes general and specialized classrooms in one wing, and shared facilities such as music, performing arts, gymnasium, and library in the other. At the junction of these two wings is a two-story commons, which opens to an outdoor U-shaped courtyard. The commons incorporates the cafeteria and is the multifunctional cultural hub of the school and the focus of the public zone. The classroom wing is broken into eight self-contained neighborhood learning clusters on one side, juxtaposed against a linear bar of specialized science and arts classrooms. In this zone, the spaces are grouped together to support the middle school team methodology, and are also flexible to allow for future change. Subdividing the school into team areas also breaks down the scale of the building, which creates a supportive environment for middle school children. The overall L-shaped configuration defines an outdoor play space onto which the classroom clusters open.

1

1 *Cafeteria/commons*

Opposite Entry arcade from north

3

4

3 *View from west*

4 *View from southeast*

5 *Level one plan*

6 *Classroom learning cluster*

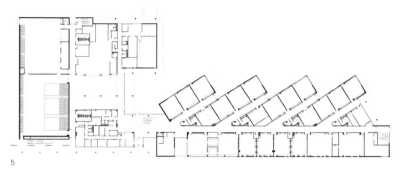

5

6

Clark County Elementary School Prototype

Las Vegas, Nevada, USA

Design completion: 2008
Construction completion: 2010
Client: Clark County School District
Area: 86,383 square feet

Perkins+Will in association with JMA Architecture participated in an invited competition to design a new elementary school that will become a prototype for new school construction in the rapidly expanding Clark County School District in Las Vegas, Nevada. The district's brief was to take a benchmark of its most recently constructed school and increase the size of the program areas by 5 to 10 percent; to reduce energy consumption by 67 percent; and to reduce construction costs by 20 percent as measured against the benchmark facility.

The building is essentially a two-story warehouse with load-bearing, insulated, tilt-up concrete perimeter walls and steel column and roof framing. The tripartite plan was suggested from construction demands and breaks a simple and efficient rectangular organization into three pieces, rotated relative to each other to create visual interest. The kindergarten is placed at one end and the school's multipurpose room at the other, with clerestory-lit entry atrium and skylit courtyard spaces providing breaks between building masses. Rollup window walls open up the art and science departments to the interior courtyard and the multipurpose room to the entry atrium, providing flexibility and expanding the educational program to the outdoors.

The design exceeded all the district's goals while providing the flexibility to adapt to future site configurations. Primary strategies included maximum controlled daylighting, ensuring that every classroom has daylight and a view. Skylight tubes, daylit courtyards, and clerestory windows help balance daylight in the classrooms and bring daylight deep into the lower levels; all windows are protected with external sunshades. The roof layout is designed to accommodate 15,000 square feet of photovoltaic panels, which will satisfy 10 percent of electrical demand, while also serving as shading devices for the interior courtyard and drop-off/arrival area. The advantages of the insulated tilt-up concrete perimeter wall are quick assembly, inexpensive durable materials, and readily available skill sets in the local market. From a thermal performance perspective, the outer concrete surface provides thermal lag, which combines with the inner insulation layer to maintain constant cool temperatures within the building. Heavy roof insulation and a "cool" reflective roof complement the envelope strategies.

1 South façade arrival court
2 Entry atrium
3 Ground floor plan

1

2

3

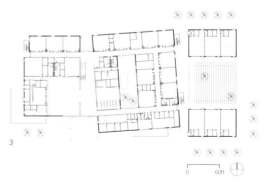

0   60ft

Hector P. Garcia Middle School

Dallas, Texas, USA

Design completion: 2005
Construction completion: 2007
Client: Dallas Independent School District
Area: 175,000 square feet

Hector P. Garcia Middle School provides a broad selection of learning opportunities and services. The 175,000 square foot school, serving 1,200 students spanning grades six through eight, is organized around three teams per grade level. The design includes academic and support spaces to support classroom instruction, sciences, technology, and world languages for traditional, interdisciplinary, and project-based instruction. A special education program is centrally located to allow special needs students to be included in the social life of the school. Supporting and encouraging practical lifelong skills, the school offers flexible and technology-enabled learning environments for career investigation, business education, and family consumer sciences.

The building's layout nurtures social and academic development in a safe and secure environment. Supporting the neighborhood and community beyond school hours, the building is zoned to allow public access to the gymnasium, library, and performing arts areas.

Located on a tight urban site, the building is situated to maximize north daylighting, while limiting solar exposure on the east and west façades. The site is organized with perimeter vehicular areas to allow uninterrupted student access to athletic and play areas. At the street level, the school provides an engaging streetscape to reinforce its role in re-invigorating the urban neighborhood environment.

The school's architectural design expresses the social organization of the program and creates an appropriate climatic response to the environment. Aesthetically, the school expresses the forward-looking educational program while reflecting Dallas' rich tradition of regional modernism. Hector P. Garcia Middle School is LEED certified.

1   North elevation of classroom bar

1

2

2 North elevation showcasing
  entry and cantilevered media
  center

3 View of south entry and
  cafeteria

4 Entry floor plan

5 Media center looking toward
  downtown Dallas

6 Main lobby

3

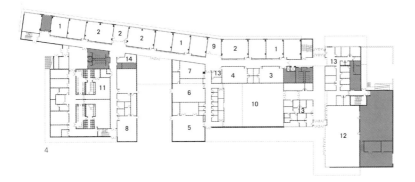

1 Classrooms
2 Science
3 Business education
4 Career education
5 Band
6 Choir
7 Drama
8 Arts
9 Resource room
10 Auditorium
11 Athletics
12 Dining
13 Administration
14 Teacher planning

Service spaces

4

5

6

Patriot High School

Riverside, California, USA

Design completion: 2002
Construction completion: 2005
Client: Jurupa Unified School District
Area: 214,000 square feet

This "urban village" scheme is represented by the dynamic arrangement of educational facilities centered around a public outdoor assembly space. The high school project consists of five separate buildings that form a well-defined building center. Most of the buildings are a steel braced-frame construction, which allows significant flexibility in the event that floor plan changes are ever required.

During the planning and design process, the Jurupa Unified School District concentrated on two primary goals: to create classrooms that are true "learning laboratories," and to explore usage possibilities by the wider community. The community facilities include a 400-seat theater with full fly loft, athletic fields/facilities, and a larger library with separate student and public entrances. The community components are easily recognizable on the campus.

Standard classrooms are increased to 1,150 square feet and feature operable walls for maximum flexibility, allowing the rooms to extend to 2,300 square foot learning environments. Every classroom can function as an art, science, or math classroom, depending on the needs of the school. This flexibility allows the school to develop an integrated educational approach and accommodate fluctuating curriculum requirements. In addition, small group environments and support spaces are located throughout the campus to support multiple types of learning, including small learning communities and departmentalized instruction.

By creating building layouts that function either as departmental classroom groupings or as grade-level groupings (small learning communities) formed around a central courtyard, the district is better able to respond to changing educational philosophies. For instance, with science labs concentrated in both classroom buildings, the science department is able to function separately, or as an integrated subject course within each grade level. In addition to the flexibility of the design, the classrooms incorporate light shelves and natural ventilation to create an environment that enhances the learning potential of the students.

1   Library

1

2

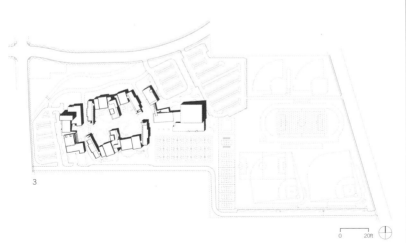

3

4

0   20ft

5

6

Perspectives Charter School
Chicago, Illinois, USA

Design completion: 2001
Construction completion: 2004
Client: Perspectives Charter School
Area: 30,000 square feet

The founders of the Perspectives Charter School coined the motto
"A Disciplined Life" to characterize its mission for an ideal school
environment. Perkins+Will's design of the school's facility integrates
the philosophy of the disciplined life with a program-specific design
response resulting in an unconventional school design.

Perspectives Charter School, housing 300 students in grades six through
twelve, is a public school located on Chicago's near south side. The
school occupies the pointed end of a triangular site created by Archer
Boulevard, leaving an entry plaza and play area to the west in what
was a former parking lot.

A raised roof element, which forms a clerestory for the central space,
engages the western face to frame a glazed entry hall and wraps down
to form an entry canopy. The tip of the triangle contains space for a
future library and is finished with an outdoor classroom and trellis.
The corrugated metal skin is an economical material that echoes the
area's industrial past.

The building reflects the unique culture that has resulted from the
hard work, vision, and dedication of the school's students, parents,
teachers, and administrators. Interaction and socialization among the
students and the staff of the school are integral to the Perspectives way
of learning and are facilitated by small group spaces and other areas
that allow for a variety of uses and interactions beyond those that occur
in the classroom. The multipurpose room is treated as a two-story
"living-room" around which the classrooms are oriented; multilingual
graphics taken from the school's mission statement decorate this space.

Through responsive planning and innovative use of materials and color,
all while working within a limited budget, the design encourages and
exemplifies the unique educational approach of the school.

1   West façade

1

2

3

4

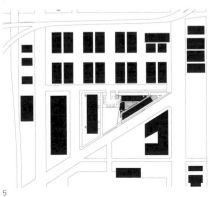

5

7

8

235 Van Buren

Chicago, Illinois, USA

Design completion: 2007
Construction completion: March 2010
Client: CMK Development Corporation
Area: 950,000 square feet

Located in the South Loop neighborhood of downtown Chicago,
235 Van Buren is a residential tower designed to work as a transition
between the more commercial developments to the north and the
residential and mixed-use developments to the south. It is also a
response to two site conditions. The first condition, to the north,
is the densely infilled context of the Chicago "Loop." The second
condition, to the south, is an open space created by a freeway
and traffic interchange that also contains a small park.

The articulation of the two masses is distinctly different to respond to
these two conditions. The southern glass façade and random balconies
provide a large-scale backdrop to the open space created by the major
traffic interchange. A ribbon of concrete frames the glass wall,
undulating to define the penthouse units and providing a large-scale
gesture to the expressway, as well as to the taller buildings to the
north. The random balconies express the individuality of the units
within, as well as providing a kinetic image from the freeway.

The northern façade is a flush grid of rectangular openings with inset
balconies. This gesture relates the building back to the historic Chicago
Loop and the frame-expressed architecture of the "Chicago School."

The overall mass of the building is broken down by dividing the tower
into two slabs. This concept reduces the scale of the building, provides
an urban space at the street corner that relates to the existing plaza on
the opposite corner, and pronounces the entry to the residences.
Making the two slabs different heights also provides relief at the top
of the building, enlivening it among the taller office towers in the vicinity.

1

1   Penthouse terrace

2   South façade

2

3

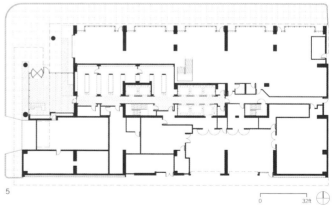

4

5

3 View from south

4 Typical residential plan

5 Level one plan

6 View from northwest

7 Entry from west

8 Exploded axonometric

0   32ft

7

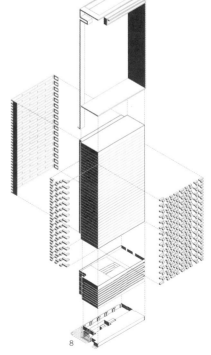

6

8

Contemporaine
Chicago, Illinois, USA

Design completion: 2001
Construction completion: 2004
Client: CMK Development Corporation
Area: 96,000 square feet

This 28-unit condominium building, consisting of an 11-story residential tower and four-story retail and parking base, is located on a corner lot in the River North area of urban Chicago.

The mass of the tower is broken down by a series of slots scored down the façade with small cantilevered balconies. The undulating east façade further breaks the mass while providing more opportunities for views of the city skyline. Two concrete shear walls and the plane of the roof frame the design and provide a distinctive profile. The top of the tower is sculpted to offer large terraces for the penthouse units and a gesture to the surrounding skyscrapers.

To bring the base to a pedestrian scale the structure of the parking garage is exposed with floor-to-ceiling glass between the floor slabs, similar to the tower above. On the north side of the building the dynamic expression of the sloped ramps leading to the upper parking levels adds relief and movement to the otherwise rectilinear structure. At the entry corner the erosion of the mass, the projection of the cantilevered balconies above, and a 45-foot column, all reinforce the urban energy of the Contemporaine's surroundings.

A narrow slot separates the base and tower, allowing necessary transfers of the building systems as the floor programs change from residential to parking. This detail also provides an aesthetic dialogue between the two elements and allows for a reading of the building as a series of combined parts of varying scales.

Typical floors at Contemporaine provide up to four condominiums with two- and three-bedrooms plans that can be combined to allow for larger units. Each unit, ranging from approximately 950 square feet to 2,700 square feet, has at least one private outdoor balcony. Open floor plans with large expanses of floor-to-ceiling glass allow natural light and dynamic views of the downtown skyline. Four penthouses on the top floors feature living spaces with 20- to 32-foot glass walls to further capture daylight and views.

The building stands out from most of its contemporaries in the city. Through simple manipulations of modern materials—the sculpted mass, dynamic resident entry, and the texture of the window mullions—the building makes a strong statement on the cityscape.

1

1   North façade
2   View from northeast

2

3 View from west

4 East façade

5 Typical floor plan

6 Level 14 penthouse terrace

7 Level 12 penthouse

8 Typical unit

6

7

8

Dockside Green

Victoria, British Columbia, Canada

Design completion: 2005 (Master plan)
Construction completion: 2008 (Phase 1)
Client: Dockside Green Ltd. Partnership (Vancity and Windmill West)
Area: 1.3 million square feet (overall development); 180,000 square feet (Phase 1)

Dockside Green is a mixed-use development on a former brownfield site in the heart of Victoria, British Columbia. When complete, the development will total 26 buildings and include residential, live/work, hotel, retail, office, light industrial uses, and numerous public amenities. With a LEED Platinum rating targeted for each building, the project is a global showcase for large-scale sustainable development.

The first phase, Synergy, completed in March 2008, is the highest-scoring LEED Platinum-certified project on record. It includes four detached buildings constructed over a common underground parking structure: a nine-story residential tower with minor commercial units on the ground floors; a two-story townhouse; a six-story building with minor commercial units on the ground floor; and a four-story residential building.

Dockside is oriented around a central greenway that runs parallel to the shoreline. Made up of a series of water ponds and bioswales, the greenway is a key feature in the development's water management system. Site stormwater flows from the buildings and ground level concourses to the greenway where it is filtered, along with treated blackwater from the on-site wastewater treatment facility, for greywater use in toilets and irrigation. This greenway also enhances the community's liveablity by providing significant public open space.

An integrated energy system ensures the development will be greenhouse gas neutral, while also providing the opportunity for the project to become a net-energy provider. The system includes a biomass gasification plant that converts locally sourced wood waste into a clean burning gas to produce heat and hot water. The biomass system, along with selling the extra biomass heat to a neighboring hotel, has rendered the project carbon neutral on a net annual basis without the purchase of green power certificates.

Synergy's many other sustainable features include an extensive water recovery treatment strategy, expected to save more than 8 million liters of water annually; rooftop gardens; a car co-op with Smart Car; and additional energy-saving features including Energy Star appliances, heat recovery ventilations units, low-E double-glazed windows, and exterior blinds on the west and south faces of each building.

1   *Master plan*

2   *Axonometric*

1

2

3

4

5

6

222

7

Signature Place
St. Petersburg, Florida, USA

Design completion: 2007
Construction completion: 2009
Client: Cantor Development
Area: 884,526 square feet

This project developed from a shared vision between Perkins+Will and
Gulf Atlantic Real Estate Companies. The triangular building soars
366 feet high with its rippling glass façade reflecting the waves below.
The shimmering tower with its sky garden redefines the St. Petersburg
skyline with a compelling level of design and architecture.

Located at the heart of St. Petersburg's busy downtown, the street-level
urban plaza offers residents, workers, and the public a park-like oasis
for relaxation and refreshment. Within the building, lush sky gardens
surrounding an infinity pool showcase an 80-foot cascading waterfall.

The project's main feature, the 35-story residential tower, is located at
the southeastern corner of the property. This location allows all of the
residential units to have open, breathtaking views to the water. A series
of unique penthouse units on the top four levels have an average size
of 3,000 to 4,000 square feet. The structure additionally houses
37,000 square feet of office space, a 37,000 square foot recreational
deck and an 11,000 square foot amenities floor.

Signature Place's creative and invigorating design is designed to place
St. Petersburg on the world stage as a great place to live and work.

1   View from northeast

1

2 View from south

3 South façade

4 Typical residential plan

5 East façade

6 Amenity roof deck

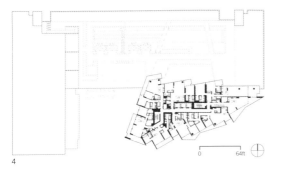

4

5

6

Skybridge

Chicago, Illinois, USA

Design completion: 2001
Construction completion: 2003
Client: Dearborn Development Company
Area: 804,000 square feet

Skybridge is a 39-story, 237-unit residential condominium tower with a five-story base component. The base consists of a grocery, bank, and coffee shop at grade, with four levels of parking above the retail.

The 425 foot tall housing slab parallels the expressway on the eastern portion of the site to maximize views of the Chicago skyline from the residential units, and to help reduce the canyon effect the tower would have on the Halsted Street side of the site. The 60-foot-tall, five-story base is a transitional element between the tower, the Halsted streetscape, and neighborhood.

The design objectives were to accommodate flexibility in unit types, combinations, value, views, and daylighting. The manipulation of mass and void, opacity and transparency create a village-like quality, as opposed to the monolithic vertical slab of many high-rise residential designs. Glass bridges span a large 30-foot-wide transparent opening, which begins at the 14th floor, forming an over-scaled urban window and suggesting an alternate reading of the building as two interconnected towers rather than a single, large mass. Beginning at the 14th floor, two units per floor are eliminated, creating a separation of the mass and ultimately providing for three additional corner units at each floor level.

The building structure is site-cast concrete, with a site-cast concrete and glass exterior enclosure. The exterior color palette is primarily light, medium, and dark shades of gray, which are used progressively from the north to the south of the building. Red, yellow, and blue are used at specific areas of articulation in the building's architectural form including entry points, at cutouts and notches in the building mass, at the slot that is created by the bridge connection between the two towers, and at specific locations that result from the erosion of the mass at the top of the building.

A major design feature of the building is at the top of the northern tower. A single four-story column supports an open roof trellis that cantilevers 40 feet above the building. This dynamic feature caps the building and acknowledges the importance of the top in relation to the surrounding towers.

1

1 *View from west*

Opposite View from northeast

4

3

The Silver Sea
Vancouver, British Columbia, Canada

Design completion: 2004
Construction completion: 2007
Client: Concord Pacific Group
Area: 55,330 square feet

This unique residential development, located between Vancouver's
Granville Street Bridge and George Wainborn Park, is designed to achieve
a high level of architectural and urban design excellence. The building
design incorporated advanced green building strategies that reduced
the level of energy and water consumption and mitigated the project's
overall environmental impact.

Suites are oriented to the south, taking advantage of views across
George Wainborn Park and False Creek. While the building is aligned
to the city grid along its north and east faces, the south-facing sides
feature a lighter, more transparent treatment. Spacious balconies
function as sunshades for floors below and are finished to express
distinct outdoor living areas and to allow interaction with the adjacent
park and marina. The building's west corner features a 1,700 square
foot commercial retail component that opens directly onto Vancouver's
sea wall walkway.

The building's stepped-back floors reflect the nautical influence of its
marina-side location. This theme is echoed in the project's landscaping,
most notably in the "moat" of collected rainwater that runs along the
building's north face. The project's sculpture and detailing serve a
similar purpose. Private entrance bridges to ground-level suites cut
through a series of island planters that contain bamboo and reeds,
aiding in water filtration for the building and site water runoff.

The Silver Sea provides an intimate connection to its surrounding marine
and park vernacular through its site, orientation, massing, form, and
materials palette. With its location at the epicenter of Vancouver's
urban model—where the tranquility of the ocean and the surrounding
density of Vancouver's downtown peninsula meet—the Silver Sea
provides a distinct addition to the neighborhood's urban fabric.

1   Waterfront view

1

3　　　　　　　4　　　　　　　5　　　　　　　6

2   Pedestrian/cyclist trail
3   Waterside balconies
4   Parkside balconies
5   View to pedestrian/cyclist trail
6   Southern sunshades
7   View from False Creek
8   Third floor plan

7

8

Arizona State University, Interdisciplinary Science & Technology Building I
Tempe, Arizona, USA

Design completion: 2004
Construction completion: 2006
Client: Arizona State University
Area: 150,000 square feet

This academic research lab is located on a university campus in Tempe, Arizona. The $52 million building houses 150,000 square feet of generic laboratories, office spaces, and support spaces, including a below-grade vivarium.

The massing of the building reflects the program with simple bar elements along the west and north sides house the flexible lab and lab support functions, while a jagged eastern wing houses office spaces.

These elements are arranged on the site to reinforce existing circulation patterns. The jagged east wing enlivens a north–south paseo, while a south-facing courtyard, formed by the three programmatic masses opens to a major east–west circulation spine to the south.

A public outdoor area is protected from the harsh sun by the mass of the office wing above and is adjacent to a landscaped courtyard contained by a low seating wall. The public area leads to a recessed double-height lobby enclosed by curtain wall protected by overhangs, as well as a small plaza at the intersection of the two wings. The plaza is shaded by the building in the mornings and afternoons, and makes use of the prevailing breezes from the southeast, which are funneled in by the shape of the building.

In dealing with the site's north–south orientation, façades respond to solar conditions while providing variety and scale to the elevations. The north is flush, overhangs protect the south, and the west is solid with protected minimum openings. The courtyard and east façades are glazed, but sheltered by a checkerboard of vertical sunscreens.

Labs and open office spaces throughout the building are situated along the checkered façades, allowing abundant natural light in, while helping to minimize glare. In the lobby, the main conference room protrudes from the level above, framed by a bamboo-paneled surround and glazed to visually link the two spaces, as well as bring in borrowed natural light. All non-support spaces and corridors within the building have natural light and views to the outside.

The mass of the concrete exterior helps reduce the impact of the desert sun on the temperature within. It also acts as a reference to regional building traditions and forms in an economic and progressive way.

The project has achieved LEED Gold certification.

1

236

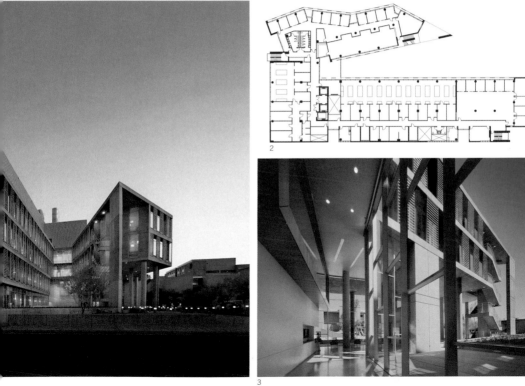

2

3

4

5

6

4   Courtyard from south
5   East façade
6   View from southwest
7   View from lab
8   View from northeast

CDC National Center for Environmental Health Building 110

Atlanta, Georgia, USA

Design completion: 2002
Construction completion: 2005
Client: Centers for Disease Control and Prevention
Area: 145,000 square feet

This modern, clear, and sustainable laboratory building sets a new architectural standard for government research facilities. A highly articulated and effective screen wall system is a major architectural expression, offering impressive views and allowing filtered daylight deep into research areas. An extraordinarily simple prismatic volume is clearly articulated in a Moebius strip of masonry and glass.

Designed to accommodate changing equipment needs and shifts in program emphasis, the design concept for this building is based on maximum flexibility and adaptability.

The building's requirements for environmental control, security, chain-of-custody, and safety create unique circumstances that must be addressed as conditions and laboratory agenda evolve. Securable by zones, the building is more than 75 percent mobile for quick response. Many post-9/11 security-related design drivers were also implemented.

Among Building 110's most unique features are its high, sloped ceilings in an open-lab layout, allowing for natural light to penetrate deep into the spaces. To admit light and create a visual connection through the public corridor, the walls separating the outer and inner lab zones have clerestory windows and the walls between the labs and public corridor are glazed. Exterior solar controls are used to minimize glare in the building.

Fixed casework is limited to fume hoods, bio safety cabinets, and sinks. The rest of the equipment and casework is flexible, including moveable tables and mobile base cabinets that can quickly be rearranged as research needs evolve. Reconfiguration flexibility is also encouraged through wet columns—one of the first applications of wet columns for a laboratory building. Additionally, overhead service carriages and docking stations promote flexibility.

This building is LEED Gold certified. The many innovative sustainable strategies included 46 percent of the building's materials sourced within 500 miles and 21 percent were recycled; HVAC condensate is captured and used for irrigation; and advanced daylighting strategies, which contribute to reduced energy costs.

1

1   Volumetric composition
    of building materials

2   Brise soleil on west lab wall

2

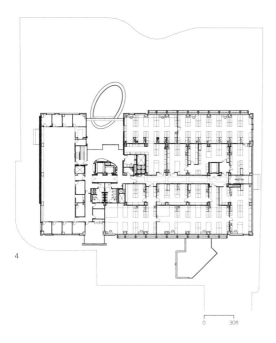

4

0   30ft

Opposite *Entry lobby*

4 *Typical floor plan*

5 *Flexible labs enhanced*
by filtered daylight

5

Interdisciplinary Life Sciences Building

College Station, Texas, USA

Design completion: 2006
Construction completion: 2009
Client: Texas A&M University
Area: 228,000 square feet

The Texas A&M University Interdisciplinary Life Sciences Building is a three-story laboratory complex constructed to enhance the University's research interactions across disciplines, including Agriculture and Life Sciences, Liberal Arts, Science, Veterinary Medicine, and Biomedical Sciences. This facility will enable A&M to recruit outstanding faculty, enhance its research reputation, and pursue major research funding. The Interdisciplinary Life Sciences Building is sited prominently across from the historic Simpson Drill Field and serves as both a physical and conceptual link between the campus' life sciences corridor to the east and its research buildings to the west.

The Interdisciplinary Life Sciences Building represents the latest thoughts in sustainable laboratory design. Labs and lab support facilities utilize modular design strategies to permit reconfiguration based on evolving research directions. The facility has achieved USGBC LEED Gold certification.

The building includes 95,000 square feet of modular laboratories and research offices to support chemical, biological and computational work. A large Microscopy and Imaging Center includes state-of-the-art electron microscopes.

Core facilities include proteomics, genomics and structural biology labs that will serve the entire University's research needs. Additional functions include a vivarium, a 300-seat auditorium, a coffee shop, and a large atrium to help foster cross-discipline collaboration.

Native Texas limestone and campus standard brick reinforce the A&M University campus aesthetic, while trellises provide both shade for pedestrians and solar control for the laboratories and offices. Natural daylighting permeates the building, including both the research atrium and lobby. Site features include both a formal lawn and a sustainable rain garden. The building's wedge shape responds to the planned life science connector corridor.

1   Old main entry elevation looking south at the Albritton Bell Tower

1

2

3

4

6

5

7

Ohlone College Newark Center for Health Sciences and Technology
Newark, California, USA

Design completion: 2006
Construction completion: 2008
Client: Ohlone Community College District
Area: 130,000 square feet

This ground-breaking Center's extensive energy-reduction systems and other sustainable design strategies resulted in it being the first campus in the United States to achieve LEED Platinum certification. The key systems employed to reduce demand and provide most of the Center's energy needs include photovoltaics, passive geothermal, and enthalpy wheels. The result is a facility that uses 31 percent of California's Title 24 Energy Use standards, and, for five months of the year, actually contributes power to the grid.

The 81-acre site is located on the southern edge of San Francisco Bay. The southern component of the project contains the nursing, allied health, biotechnology, environmental sciences, and the exercise and wellness programs, as well as administration. The northern component contains general education classrooms, computer and information technology, information services, contract education, student services, and a learning resource center. The two wings are joined by the campus commons featuring a bookstore, cafe, scholarly activity, and training areas. With smart classrooms and flexible laboratory spaces throughout, the Newark Center is built to evolve as community needs change.

The building's orientation and shape, as well as the design of its roof overhangs, respond to operational and climatic conditions, with massing that buffers occasional high winds. Roofs combine metal and membrane as "folded planes" that extend to provide shade on sunny days and drape over the building edge to form rain screens during inclement weather. The building's form is tailored to meet the Center's instructional and service needs, with circulation routes in and around the building arranged to promote interaction.

The enthalpy wheels help provide the benefits of operable windows without dust, dirt, noise, or energy loss, with a 300 percent increase in fresh air delivery. Large windows allow views into the spinning enthalpy wheels with a status/instructional panel immediately adjacent to the window. Near the entry, public computers display the sustainable elements of the design including real-time calculation of solar power being generated. A wetland at the southern end of the campus is being restored by the environmental science students and faculty.

1

4

Sanford-Burnham Medical Research Institute at Lake Nona

Orlando, Florida, USA

Design completion: 2007
Construction completion: 2009
Client: Tavistock
Area: 178,000 square feet

The Sanford-Burnham Medical Research Institute focuses on several areas of exploration: cancer research, neuroscience, aging research, as well as infectious and inflammatory diseases. At Sanford-Burnham, a collaborative style of research is promoted, bringing together biologists, chemists, biophysicists, engineers, and computer scientists.

The project has two parallel wings with a connecting hub. The larger wing contains the research laboratory and vivarium while the smaller wing contains the conference center, administrative offices, and cafeteria. The wings are joined by a two story glass-walled common space. The three floors of research space are connected by a series of stairs that facilitate direct circulation and communication among the scientists from the various disciplines. The administrative wing has direct access to the common space, which opens to a landscaped courtyard. The cafeteria overlooks the adjacent double helix water feature. The building's expression portrays Sanford-Burnham's commitment to healing through research, along with its dedication to progressive research and sustainability.

Security was a key issue and strategies included the provision for consistent monitoring of individual occupants, which is vital given the sensitive nature of the research undertaken at the Institute. Perkins+Will coordinated the security criteria so that they became intertwined with the project's infrastructure and architecture.

The site employs several sustainable design strategies to enhance the local environment. Two large bioswales surround the site, receiving storm water runoff and reducing its suspended solids before it infiltrates the soil. The landscape design employs plant species that are either adaptive or native to the site, helping achieve a projected 50 percent reduction in total water applied for landscaping irrigation. Energy recovery, substantial reduction in process water use, rainwater recapture, cutting-edge sputtered low-e coating on exterior glazing, and responsible choices of interior finish materials are some of the other strategies employed in this project. Tropical design strategies included harnessing prevailing winds for cooling collaborative areas, and custom curtain wall overhangs placed on building façades to maximize the amount of shading on the glazed surfaces.

This building is LEED Gold certified.

1 *View across lake from northeast*

1

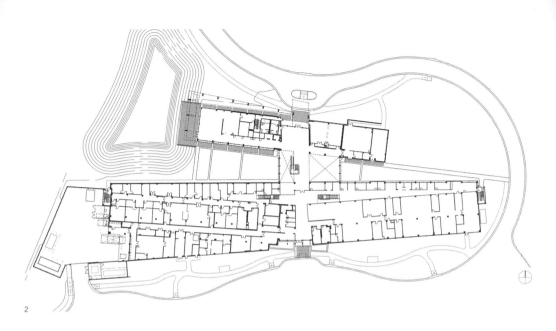

2

3

4

5

Wallis Annenberg Research Center

Los Angeles, California, USA

Design completion: 2005
Construction completion: 2007
Client: House Ear Institute
Area: 24,000 square feet

This project expands the research program of the House Ear Institute, home of the internationally renowned organization focused on hearing and the ear. The project provides two floors of new wet labs, a bio-containment lab, lab support, dedicated "core" areas, and associated offices to support the research mission of the Cellular and Molecular Medicine Division. The plan concept of the building, inspired by the curvilinear shape of the cochlea of the inner ear, creates and defines a new outdoor space and arrival courtyard. The research functions are housed on the second and third floors, the ground floor houses flexible expansion space, and the basement level contains building support and vehicular access to an existing subterranean parking structure.

Reception and arrival to the new wing are via the third floor of the existing building. A circulation concourse along the north-facing curved glass wall provides views to the Hollywood Hills and access to the labs, offices, open work areas, and conference rooms. Labs are arranged along the south side of the building and enjoy natural daylighting modulated by light shelf reflector/sunshades. Researcher offices with operable windows are positioned along the western surface, which is shaded by a projecting aluminum sunscreen. The acute-angled "prow" of the building contains conference rooms on each floor. A centrally located open stairway facilitates spontaneous interaction and communication among researchers and connects the two lab floors, promoting a team culture.

The tiered, curvilinear glazed wall on the north defines an outdoor arrival court and provides views from the open work areas, conference rooms, and the circulation concourse to the adjacent mountains. The resulting outdoor "room" below contains spaces for reflection amid renovated gardens and provides access to a new glass-canopied entry to the building. The south and west elevations are clad with fluted precast concrete—simultaneously matching the new building to the existing building in terms of material and color, while the form, texture, and detailing of the paneling sets it apart with a strong, dynamic new identity.

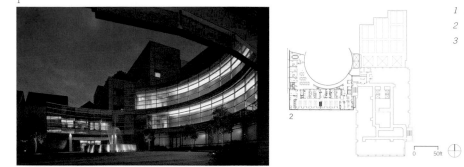

1   Arrival court
2   Third floor plan
3   "Prow" viewed from
     intersection

0   50ft

ON THE BOARDS PROJECTS

Atlanta BeltLine Corridor Design

Atlanta, Georgia, USA

Design completion: 2011
Estimated construction completion: 2030
Client: Atlanta BeltLine, Inc.
Area: 300 acres

The Atlanta BeltLine is an ambitious vision for the future of the city's intown communities, allowing them to significantly expand their population, employment, and services while maintaining their quality of life. The BeltLine is a 22-mile transit greenway circling the central city that reuses a loop of underutilized railroads. The wide linear park will feature streetcars, bicycle and pedestrian paths, and connect over 40 diverse neighborhoods, as well as city schools, historic and cultural sites, shopping districts, and public parks. It organizes more than 174 million square feet of adjacent underutilized urban land for transit-oriented development, expands transit service within the urban core, and connects various parts of an emerging regional trail system. It takes advantage of Atlanta's intown population growth, creating smart new districts for more than 100,000 new residents and improved quality of life for hundreds of thousands more.

Originating as a master's thesis project at Georgia Tech, and supported by a tremendous groundswell of public support, the core proposal of transit, trail, and economic development has expanded to include new parks, affordable housing, public art, historic preservation, an arboretum and many other ideas both large and small. With district planning, adjacent park designs and other work underway, the BeltLine Corridor Design establishes the BeltLine's vision in physical space and in three dimensions, defining the specific means of physical expression that will create something greater than anything anyone has imagined to date.

Perkins+Will is leading this effort, teamed with James Corner Field Operations and a team of consultants who bring expertise in all disciplines. The Corridor Design is Atlanta's primary opportunity to ensure that the project's implementation over time will accomplish all of the BeltLine's promise through a functional, elegant, groundbreaking, and cohesive urban design. It will establish the integrated design relationships between the transit, trail, and other core components. It will formally embed supporting design strategies such as art, preservation, signage, and the arboretum into the BeltLine's design. It will ensure that the grand vision is also sustainable, efficient, and affordable to build and operate. Finally, this framework design will deliver the greatest promise of the BeltLine: it will support, protect, and enhance the quality of life for the city of Atlanta through the next several decades of dramatic regional transformation.

1   Transit, trail and greenway
    functions layered throughout
    the BeltLine

2   Transforming underutilized
    but valuable urban land

Calexico West Border Station

Calexico, California, USA

Design completion: 2011
Estimated construction completion: 2014
Client: General Services Administration (GSA)
Area: 117,000 square feet of buildings and 138,000 square feet of canopies

Paired with Mexicali MX just south of the border, the Calexico port of entry architecture, landscape, and infrastructure will create an intersection of specific environment, rich culture, and civic pride, and will aspire to the highest level of design innovation and creativity. The port of entry will be successful if it can be at once bold and ordinary, authentic without being novel, and simple in appearance but complex in content and meaning. To the highest degree this place should be an organism of the environment, doing no harm, using the sun, wind, water, and land responsibly.

There are three primary buildings: the pedestrian port of entry building, the central administration building, and the vehicle port of entry building.

Starting at the east end of the site, the pedestrian building is one story tall with a basement. The building houses pedestrian primary and secondary inspection. Primary inspection occurs in a glazed space with a high ceiling.

At the center of the site is the central administration building, a three-story structure with a basement. It houses the central detention unit, employee support spaces, and agency offices. It is a boomerang-shaped building, with a single story east-west wing that is tucked under a landform to the south and opens to a landscaped cut to the north. The other wing of the building is three stories, with the southern end of the building cantilevering over the landform.

At the vehicle port of entry there is a pre-primary canopy, a canopy at the primary inspection booths, and a secondary canopy. At the basement level under the roadway between the primary and secondary canopies is a space for a future southbound secondary inspection area. To the west is a southbound inspection booth with a canopy and employee parking.

The buildings are tied together with a shaped landscape that rises as high as the top of the first story on the eastern buildings and generally faces south. To the north on either side of the railroad tracks the site is excavated one story down to bring light into the basement level and create private courts accessible from the buildings. At the basement level the pedestrian building and administration building are linked by a tunnel under the railroad tracks.

1   Overview of site

2   Northbound pedestrian pavilion

1

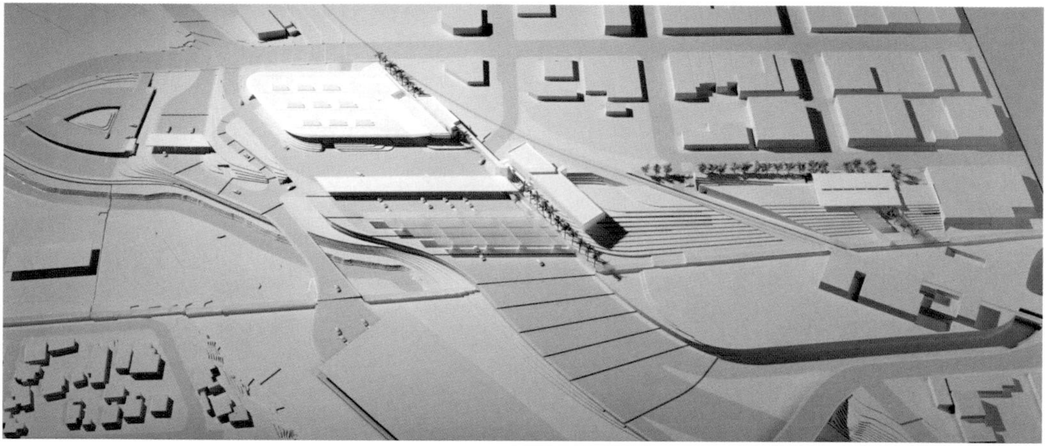

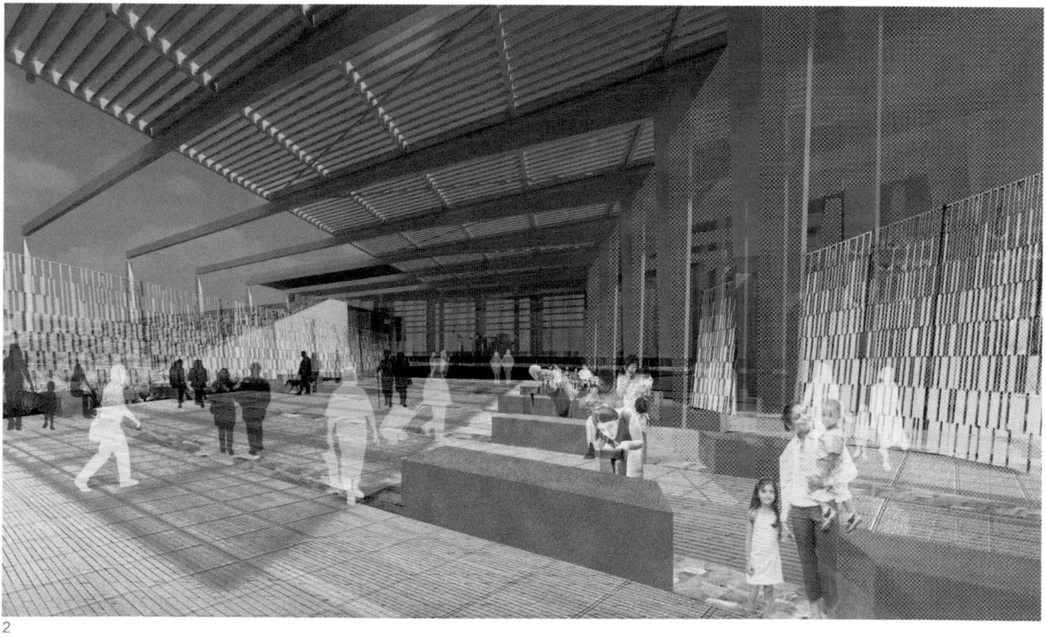

2

Desertcreat College

Cookstown, Northern Ireland

Design completion: 2011
Estimated construction completion: 2012
Client: Police Service of Northern Ireland
Area: 586,000 square feet, with an additional 1.2 million square feet of training villages

Desertcreat College is a new integrated academic and practical training campus for the Police, Prison, and Fire and Rescue services of Northern Ireland. The project site is a gently rolling 278 acre zone of agricultural fields and woodland in the geographic center of the province of Ulster. The Killymoon, an ecologically significant river, runs through the site from west to east.

The site development strategy proposes a constructed campus ecosystem oriented west to east that parallels the natural corridor of the Killymoon River. Ecologically sensitive areas to the north of the river are set aside for lighter impact practical training uses. The academic campus and the principal shared and public functions of the campus are at the center of the site. To the south are the practical training areas for the three uniformed services.

The "sheltered campus" concept proposes a unifying roof structure in dialogue with the landscape, under which the academic campus buildings are assembled and protected. The concept integrates the built environment with the landscape, protects from threats, allows for natural ventilation, visually unifies the campus buildings, and creates a strong campus identity.

The project is on target to achieve carbon neutrality by reducing energy consumption through the use of passive ventilation in all classrooms and office spaces; on-site willow harvesting for heat generation with a bio-mass boiler, and on-site electrical generation with a wind turbine. The landscape design proposes new stands of native woodland, new native grasslands, new native wetland to augment existing habitats, and willow coppicing to enhance biodiversity.

1   *Welcome center*

2   *Academic campus*

3   *Main entry and service exhibit hall*

1

2

3

LA Courthouse

Los Angeles, California, USA

Design completion: 2001
Client: General Services Administration (GSA)
Area: 1 million square feet

With its sweeping 16-story curvilinear curtain wall oriented toward City Hall, the new Los Angeles Federal courthouse is a dialogue between modern architectural forms and the particularity of its Civic Center context. The building massing is an abstract distillation of four icons of traditional American courthouse design: the portal, the column, the rotunda, and the cupola. Reaching beyond monumentality to express the inherent dignity of the courts and the fundamental democratic view of the importance of the individual, this urban building—with a refined, transparent structure and "civic garden" of intimate spaces—celebrates both openness and human scale.

The design draws its inspiration and form from Los Angeles' most prominent historic building—City Hall—and from late 19th-century courthouses. The 1928 City Hall is a hybrid of two influences. The base recalls a classical pavilion, a universally accepted symbol of government architecture, and the tower recalls the skyscraper, which at the time, was an evolving building type from the private sector. Late 19th-century courthouses in hot, dry climates used towers not only as symbolic focal points but also to function as thermal vents. The tower facilitated convection by drawing hot air out the top of the building while drawing cool air in from the bottom. This scheme adopts a similar approach by blending abstracted classical iconography (columns and portals) with sustainable contemporary technology from the private sector (a large south-facing curtain wall solar collector and a thermal cupola). Together these provide a strong but accessible image for the courthouse, while creating a model sustainable design.

The proposed project involves the construction of a one million square foot courthouse, with at least 150 enclosed parking spaces. The facility would be constructed to meet 10-year requirements of the District Court and court-related agencies on a site large enough to accommodate a 30-year expansion plan. The courthouse is currently scheduled to include a minimum of 54 District and Magistrate courtrooms.

With a goal to achieve LEED Silver, the design incorporates light shelves that harvest daylight from both ends of the courtroom; a south facing atrium that contains integrated photovoltaic panels; and primary mechanical ventilation that is delivered via an under-floor air distribution system.

1 Atrium

2 Model from northeast

3 View from southeast

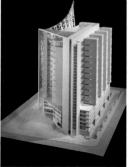

Musée de Louvain-la-Neuve

Louvain-la-Neuve, Belgium

Design completion: 2009
Estimated completion completion: 2012
Client: Louvain-la-Neuve
Area: 54,000 square feet

The design of this museum was driven by the concept of a building that would both preserve and create a new park-like setting along an existing lake while simultaneously acting as an entrance element in the context of the campus' masterplan.

The building consists of two major elements: an exhibition tower that houses the museum's permanent art collection, offices, and workshops, and a park-covered base that contains public functions such as a theme bar, auditorium, and temporary exhibition space, as well as extending the landscape over the roof. The exhibition tower grows out of the landscape via a sloping green roof and forms an edge along the boulevard while creating a more intimate and natural setting at the lakeside.

Each façade responds, contextually and sustainably, to the specific orientations of the site. The north side is a fully glazed channel glass system with transparent openings at strategic locations to allow natural light into the gallery spaces. The southern "living wall" is a more solid element that inhibits direct sunlight from entering the galleries while enhancing the naturalistic setting along the lakeside.

1   View from southwest

2   Central exhibition space

3   Level one plan

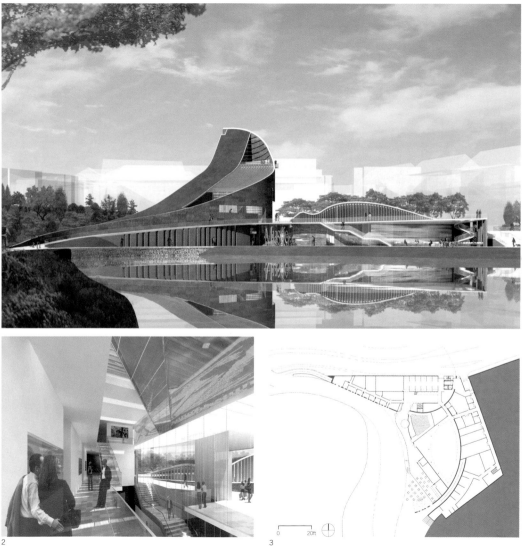

1

2

3

Shanghai Nature Museum
Shanghai, People's Republic of China

Design completion: 2009
Estimated construction completion: 2011
Client: Shanghai Science & Technology Museum
Area: 474,000 square feet

This museum sits on an urban site, adjacent to a proposed sculpture park. The shape and internal organization of the building are inspired by the form of the nautilus shell. A spiraling grass-covered plane rises out of the sculpture park and wraps around an oval pond, which is the central visual focus of the exhibition route through the building. The landscape and public plazas of the new museum are designed to be integral with the adjacent sculpture park, while also providing a unique experience for the visitor.

Three concepts were at the core of the museum design: the first concept is the introduction of plant groupings, called "primordial forests." These consist of wild and untamed planted landforms edged with granite rocks, which are dispersed throughout the site. These landforms are part of the learning experience of the museum as well as acting as seating areas and social spaces.

The second concept is the introduction of an "oval pool." Recognizing that 71 percent of the earth's surface is covered by water, this element becomes the central focus of the scheme. Water provides movement, sound, and reflections, with waves, ripples and patterns as part of the museum experience.

The third concept is "tectonic plates." Paving composed of multi-directional stone patterns recall the tectonic plates of the earth. This surface acts as a tabula rasa of the scheme since the museum is set on this stone platform, which also penetrates into the ground-floor interior spaces and under the oval water pool.

The three main façades of the building also express the message of the exhibits. The structural network and sunscreen that lines the curved inner face of the building is both an abstraction of patterns found in traditional pavilions and a suggestion of human cell organization. The north wall, which is the group-entry façade along the bus drop-off, suggests the shifting of tectonic plates. The east wall is a living wall plane covered with hydroponic planting trays, representing the vegetation of the earth's surface. With the natural landscape groupings, these features focus our awareness on the fundamental elements of the natural world: plants, earth, and water.

1   View from southwest

2   Central courtyard

3   Entry from southeast

Tianjin Museum
Tianjin, People's Republic of China

Design completion: 2009
Client: Tianjin Design Service Co. Ltd.
Area: 538,000 square feet

The Tianjin Museum, the New Natural History Museum, Art Museum, and Library are organized along a cultural corridor within the master plan that is inspired by the founding of Tianjin as the "Land of the Heavenly Ford." The buildings are sited as a sequence of water passages, gardens, and plazas that engage the public as they pass through the site.

Each cultural building incorporates a unique plaza as both an educational device and public interaction space. The Tianjin Museum's City plaza presents the layers of Tianjin history as an occupiable plaza of green space, water, and seating at the lake level, while being an educational device that interacts with the City View Window at the upper level of the museum. Similarly the Art Museum incorporates a large art plaza and the library a grand Knowledge plaza, representing a contrast of the written words housed within the library and the temporary interaction of the public.

The museum concept is based on an abstraction of a series of historical elements relating to the founding of Tianjin. The water and pedestrian walkways surrounding the museum recall the saltern beds that were part of the salt industry, still one of Tianjin's major industries. The crystalline form of salt is also the inspiration for the façade system and atrium. The "Crystal Atrium" forms the grand hall and rises above the lower scale massing of the main building as a focal point while the façade system consists of individual cast translucent glass cubes that will react with natural lighting conditions to enliven the presence of the museum within its context. The uplifted form of the museum's entry recalls the first modern operable bridge that was located in Tianjin. The bridges in the atrium also recall the traditional pedestrian bridges in the city's historical structure.

The galleries are organized around the atrium so that the visitor can interact with the exhibits in a variety of thematic or chronological ways. The Tianjin window is a focal point of the various exhibit sequences and also provides views of the old city and the Tianjin City plaza below.

1   *Exploded axonometric*

2   *View from northeast*

3   *View from northeast*

4   *Central exhibition space*

5   *View from southwest*

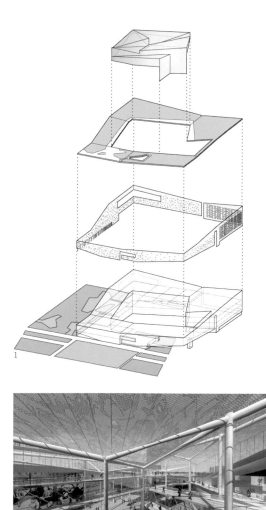

1

2

3

4

5

Al-Birr Foundation Office Tower

Riyadh, Saudi Arabia

Design completion: 2007
Estimated construction completion: 2015
Client: Al-Birr Foundation
Area: 590,000 square feet

This new headquarters building explores the typology of an urban tower in the extreme environmental conditions of Riyadh through a reinterpretation of three iconic elements of Islamic culture: the spiral minaret, the walled garden, and the mashrabiya.

The design begins with a simple rectangular form from which a unique spatial and formal identity is created. As a major tower in Riyadh, this 28-story building extends the central axis of the city, which is currently defined by low and mid-rise structures. A "spiraling garden" is carved from the volume of the rectangle, creating a continuous spatial sequence with a series of open terraces that serve as hanging courtyard gardens for the building occupants. The enclosing skin creates varying levels of openness based on solar exposure and spatial and contextual influences. Evoking the traditional mashrabiya latticework screen, this permeable skin creates a delicate balance of static and dynamic expression.

The building's orthogonal floor plates simplify office configuration and construction methodology while allowing the dynamic section to animate the spatial quality of the building. The garden terraces create temperate microclimatic environments through convective air movement and evaporative cooling enhanced by localized water-misting. The tower's intricate enclosure is formed of lightweight glass-impregnated photo-catalytic precast concrete supplemented with fly-ash. Beyond structurally supporting the tower, it controls solar and heat gain, frames dramatic views to the city, and functions as a light shelf to help distribute daylight deep into the building. Calibrated to the changing sun angles, the perforated northern elevation allows for views and cooling breezes, and transitions to a primarily opaque condition at the southern elevation. Illuminated internally at night, the enclosure's varying apertures result in a distinctive pattern of light, an inversion of the solar-regulating function of the tower enclosure during the day.

The design for the Al-Birr Foundation Headquarters inverts the relationship of skin versus support, simultaneously protecting, revealing, and embodying the activity within. Ultimately, the building offers a new paradigm for high-rise design in hot/dry climates through an integrated response to context, climate, and culture.

1 Building section
2 Lobby interior
3 View looking southeast

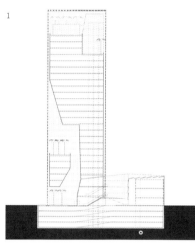

1

2

3

Merchant Square

London, England

Design completion: 2008
Estimated construction completion: 2011
Client: European Land and Properties
Area: 1.4 million square feet

Located in Paddington basin, at the heart of London's West End, Merchant Square is part of a large urban redevelopment plan along the southeast branch of the Grand Union Canal. The six proposed buildings at Merchant Square form the central focus of a dynamic mixed-use master plan for this former industrial and warehouse district. Three commercial, two mid-rise residential buildings, and a 43-story residential tower are planned for the site.

The landmark building of the development is the tower, a thin free-standing object composed of a stepped vertical volume and a glazed shield. The main volume has expressed floor lines, variegated opaque and transparent glass panels, and inset balconies to provide scale and texture and to express the individuality of the residential units. The glazed shield is a minimally detailed vertical transparent plane that unifies the individually expressed floors of the main volume. It also terminates the public plaza and animates the skyline. Photovoltaic cells integrated into this south-facing element provide a portion of the required building energy and shading from southern exposure for the flats, while simultaneously adding a dynamic texture to the façade.

The two commercial buildings along the southeast of the site are conceived as backdrops to the public square. Each building has a unique architectural response to the adjacent site elements. Glass fins along the public plaza form a large-scale public artwork, which presents itself from specific viewpoints across the site by the technique of anamorphosis, a process in which a two-dimensional abstract pattern (horizontal lines) is overlaid on the three-dimensional perspective view of the building. Balconies provide outdoor breakout spaces along the canal and public square, while an alternating rhythm of two- and three-story atria visually engage the expressway and harness the daylight from the north. The atria are clad with a transparent cable-supported curtainwall and have multi-colored interior surrounds that together form a tectonically expressive series of large-scale kaleidoscopic picture windows.

1 View from northeast

2 View from north

3 View from south

4 Site plan

5 View from south

1

2

3

4

5

Oriental Fisherman's Wharf

Shanghai, People's Republic of China

Design completion: 2009
Estimated construction completion: 2012
Client: Shanghai Oriental Fisherman's Wharf Development Company
Area: 2 million square feet

Located on the Huangpu River in the Yangpu district of Shanghai, the Oriental Fisherman's Wharf project is one of the new developments planned for the World Exposition 2010. Phase one of the proposed 2 million square foot project is composed of four unique buildings sitting on top of a three-story infrastructure plinth. The buildings include a 40-story office and hotel tower, a seven-story themed retail destination, a four-story retail market, and the renovation of an existing waterfront warehouse. Below-grade infrastructure development includes two levels of parking, a subway station, and an extensive retail promenade beneath the 410,000 square foot site.

Designed as an architectural showpiece for Shanghai, the buildings reflect the long history of fishing and the fishing industry in China. The project development resulted in several unique design opportunities. The master plan is designed to connect the people of Shanghai to the previously walled-off riverfront. The building massing provides a unique architectural experience not witnessed on the Huangpu riverfront and reciprocally creates a world-class shopping, entertainment, hospitality, and culinary destination.

Overall, the project is a catalyst for re-development of this former industrial district. The winning competition master plan included phase one as well as future phases two and three.

1   View from southwest

1

Saadiat Marina SM5-11

Abu Dhabi, United Arab Emirates

Design completion: 2008
Estimated construction completion: 2011
Client: ACTG Development
Area: 723,000 square feet

The proposed Abu Dhabi 2030 Master Plan envisions a fully sustainable, carbon-neutral nation. The Saadiat Marina is a proposed mixed-use project, strongly influenced by a modified form of performance-based zoning, which established the site massing and other aspects of the urban design. Within these constraints, and based greatly on traditional cultural and historic influences, the architectural concept envisions "courtyards in the sky." Set on a multi-functional plinth, the residential units are of two types: traditional single-story flats and stacked duplex units that span between the floors. This arrangement permits the duplex units to be accessed through open vertical courtyards.

The exterior architecture reflects the idea of a vertical community and each of the residential units expresses a certain degree of individuality set within a collective framework. This approach reinforces the traditional character and urban vocabulary of the historic precincts of Abu Dhabi. Sculpture, color, light, and vegetation are utilized to pattern the façades and animate the sky courtyards. The project, in addition to being carbon neutral, includes design features capable of achieving LEED Platinum certification. The combination of green public energy sources, the availability of convenient multi-modal transportation systems, high efficiency infrastructure, and specific site and building design initiatives further enhance this project's ability to meet and even exceed performance objectives.

The plinth, or building podium, is designed to fully animate the streetscape with retail, street-oriented offices, and other pedestrian-focused functions. The highly "charged" surface of the podium fully conceals the parking ramp, which is consistent with the zoning requirements. There is even the possibility of including townhouse-type residential units on the street level.

The Saadiat Marina takes a creative approach to achieving two important urban objectives: providing vibrant pedestrian activity on the street level while avoiding the anonymous environments of large urban high-rise residential blocks. Thus, not only is the architecture sustainable, but so is the lifestyle.

1   View from south

1

Rush University Medical Center, Campus Transformation Project

Chicago, Illinois, USA

Design completion: 2010
Estimated construction completion: 2012
Client: Rush University Medical Center
Area: 750,000 square feet

This project includes a new 750,000 square foot hospital facility
including a state-of-the-art emergency department, an orthopedics
ambulatory care building, state-of-the-art emergency department,
and a centralized power plant. The current Atrium, Kellogg, and
Professional Office buildings are slated for intensive renovations
upon the completion of the new hospital. The new hospital bed tower
will include 304 acute and critical care beds, 76 NICU beds, and
10 labor delivery beds. The new hospital bed tower will also feature
roof-top gardens and is targeted for LEED Silver certification.

A key component of the new hospital will be the interventional
platform concept. Two floors extending from the new hospital into
the renovated Atrium building will be exclusively devoted to surgery,
imaging, and specialty procedures. With interventional radiology,
cardiology, and neurosurgery facilities and equipment nearby, it
will help foster collaboration and a multi-disciplinary approach for
specialists performing similar procedures. The co-location of these key
services will also minimize the need for patients and their families to
travel to multiple locations within the medical center. This innovative
concept is important to Rush's goal of reorienting its facilities and
campus around the patient.

1   View from northwest
2   Entry pavilion
3   View from southwest

Shanghai Eastern Hepatobiliary Hospital

Shanghai, People's Republic of China

Design completion: 2009
Client: Shanghai Eastern Hepatobiliary Hospital
Area: 2,152,782 square feet

The new Shanghai Eastern Hepatobiliary Hospital and National Liver Cancer Research Center have provided an opportunity to create a large healthcare precinct. The Gupu River runs through the heart of the proposed site, challenging the design to link operations and to provide integrated patient services. The design is divided into two distinct areas —the east campus and the west campus.

In the west campus at the end of a public concourse are the heath check clinics, rehabilitation department, and hospital administration and education departments. A residential component is located to the north while the research campus, including the laboratories, lab administration, and vivariums, are located to the west.

The east campus contains the outpatient clinics, emergency department, surgery and diagnostic departments, intensive care unit, and acute patient wards, as well as hospital logistics and public and staff parking. Expansion is planned along the north side of the inpatient hospital area.

Located in the east campus and very visible from primary roads, the inpatient hospital is anchored by a two-level diagnostic, treatment, and outpatient clinic block. Multiple inpatient nursing units are positioned atop the diagnostic, treatment, and outpatient clinic and cantilever over its edges. A public concourse made up of pedestrian walkways and gardens runs through the heart of the two-level block. This concourse provides a "spine" that crosses the Gupu River, linking the hospital and outpatient clinics on the east to the health check and rehabilitation facilities on the west. Situated between the main entry and a series of courtyards are four service cores with multiple elevators for dedicated visitor, patient, and materials use.

The design takes into account many symbolic and environmental considerations, including: using mounds and ponds to create a representation of the natural world inside the hospital; having gardens oriented to the south with geometric shapes representing the harmony between man and the universe; an awareness of having a spatial flow between east and west; using a combination of natural and created materials in construction; shaping the landscape to create ponds which then act as a rainwater retention system; creating a green roof to improve air quality and reduce storm water runoff and energy loss; and using recycled materials.

1   *View from west*

2   *Bed tower garden*

3   *Entry*

4   *Clinical waiting room*

1

3

2

4

Spaulding Rehabilitation Hospital

Boston, Massachusetts, USA

Design completion: 2010
Estimated construction completion: 2012
Client: Spaulding Rehabilitation Hospital
Area: 380,000 square feet

Spaulding Rehabilitation Hospital is one of the world's preeminent rehabilitation hospitals with a mission to deliver quality patient care, conduct cutting-edge research, and offer the best teaching programs available in the field. Situated along Boston Harbor in historic Charlestown Navy Yard, Spaulding's new facility is designed to be regenerative and sustainable in every aspect by promoting the health of the environment, community and patients.

The new building is clad in profiled metal panel and glass to provide an uplifting architectural expression, and to recall the site's unique history as a major ship-building center for the United States Navy from the 1800s through the early 1970s. Sunshades are integrated at larger glass expanses and a series of metal bands wrap the primary architectural volumes into a single, unified element. A masonry base anchors the building to the surrounding site and also reflects the brick tradition of Charlestown Navy Yard.

A three-story podium houses many of the hospital's common patient, public, and operational functions including; lobby, conference center, cafe, therapy pool, and gymnasiums. Administrative offices, outpatient programs and research space are also located in the podium. Landscaped roof terraces and green roofs provide both visual and physical access for patients and staff to the outdoors. This, together with a landscape design that incorporates spaces for outdoor dining, therapy, and relaxation, extends Spaulding's mission across the entire site.

The five-story tower is set back from the harbor and houses 132 private patient rooms with various specialties including spinal cord injury, traumatic brain injury, and pediatrics. Multi-purpose rooms on floors four through eight provide patients with spectacular views of the Boston city skyline.

The significant sustainable design features incorporated into the new facility include brownfield site remediation, exterior envelope optimization, natural ventilation, high-efficiency mechanical systems, cogeneration, accommodation for future alternative energy sources, water conservation, sustainable materials, and passive survivability measures, as well as ample access to nature, daylight, and views for patients and staff.

2

1 View from harbor
2 Therapy gymnasium
3 Typical inpatient floor

College of Arts at Sabah Al-Salem University City–Kuwait University

Sabah Al-Salem University City, Kuwait

Design completion: 2010
Estimated construction completion: 2014
Client: Sabah Al-Salem University
Area: 1.2 million square feet

Kuwait's climate, which features temperatures ranging from 40 to
140 degrees Fahrenheit and prevalent sandstorms, served as a primary
driver for the design for these two buildings. The design concept looked
to the diwaniya tent, a traditional gathering place and desert shelter,
for ideas of passive sustainability. The tent's social function, materiality,
form, and environmental performance are sophisticated responses to the
specific environmental and cultural conditions of the region; the tent
is also an appropriate metaphor for the spirit and function of a college
of liberal arts, a place of gathering to exchange ideas.

The first layer of the building's exterior emulates woven tent fabric with
limestone "threads;" the second interior thermal vision layer allows views
outside between the threads. The dimensions vary to accommodate the
illumination requirements of the spaces inside. The mass of the building
is lifted off the ground, with a planted buffer zone around the entire
perimeter, punctuated by a series of naturally ventilated "tent gardens"
that extend the full height of the structure.

The interior spaces are successively climate controlled, first naturally
with shade and evapotranspiration in the entry sequence and informal
gathering spaces, then moving gradually to fully conditioned in the
building's core classrooms and offices. The tent gardens, with openings
at the roof to admit controlled daylight, function as both vertical
circulation and gathering spaces, where students, teachers, and staff
can collect and interact.

The project's goal is to achieve LEED-NC Gold certification.

1   South façade

2   Exhibit Hall Tent Garden

3   Galleria Tent Garden

4   Interior of Galleria Tent Garden

College of Education at Sabah Al-Salem University City–Kuwait University

Sabah Al-Salem University City, Kuwait

Design completion: 2010
Estimated construction completion: 2014
Client: Sabah Al-Salem University
Area: 1.2 million square feet

The University's goals for the College of Education project included the creation of a strong, individual identity for the college within the multi-college master plan; a student-centered environment that would foster a community of learning; and a highly sustainable design with daylight in all classrooms, offices, and main circulation spaces. Kuwait's large swings in temperature—from 40 to 140 degrees Fahrenheit—and relative humidity—from 5 to 85 percent—challenged the design team to find innovative ways to balance community and comfort with low energy use and environmental sensitivity.

The design solution creates two five-story rectangular buildings containing modular, repetitive learning spaces that are juxtaposed against a free-form, undulating "boardwalk" enclosing a variety of learning support spaces (lounges, group study niches, and computer stations). The boardwalk is carved through the length and height of the structures, connecting all floors and functions. The interplay of solid and void between the mass of the buildings and the meandering of the boardwalk define the architectural identity of the college. It also demonstrates the belief that classroom-based learning must be complemented by an equally vital instructional support environment in which learning continues beyond the doors of the classroom.

Accessed from the boardwalk, a series of large, internal, garden courtyards—"oases"—function as major amenity nodes for the college. They are filled with daylight, sheathed in greenery, and are highly visible from the educational spaces that surround them.

The building's self-shading skin has been calibrated to its specific solar exposure to maximize daylight penetration but minimize both solar heat gain and glare. The addition of a ground glass diffusing fin at each window captures and disperses daylight deep into each learning space while contributing to solar protection. Inspired by traditional patterned screens, whose twin functions were to shade the interior while providing screened views outward, the college uses computer technology to maximize protected views from within the building while minimizing the sun's adverse effects on the building's energy performance.

The project is expected to achieve LEED-NC Gold certification when complete in 2014.

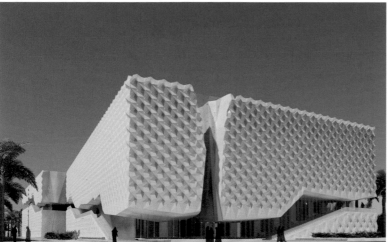

1

2

3

4

5

1   Building overview
2   Boardwalk interior
3   Detail of boardwalk and façade
4   Interior of typical classroom
5   Library interior

Florida International University Academic Health Sciences Center

Miami, Florida, USA

Design completion: under development
Estimated construction completion: 2012
Client: Florida International University
Area: 2.6 million square feet

The Academic Health Sciences Center occupies an area in the northeast corner of Florida International University's Modesto A. Maidique campus in Miami. Programs planned within the precinct include the Colleges of Medicine, Nursing and Health Sciences, and Arts and Sciences, as well as the Schools of Public Health and Social Work.

The concept for this center was to develop a coherent and identifiable campus that will enhance the personal and interactive relationship between the clinical, educational, and research components students undertake. Facilities will be designed to be efficient and flexible, to allow quick and effective responses to the rapidly changing market environment of an academic health sciences center and the health care industry.

One of the exemplary facilities, the Stempel Complex, is to become the signature entry portal to the FIU Health Science Campus. It represents the institution's commitment to being a health provider to the local community and the region. It combines three distinct yet related programs in one facility: the Robert Stempel College of Public Health and Social Work (SCPH), the Miami-Dade County Health Department (MDCHD), and the FIU Herbert Wertheim College of Medicine's Ambulatory Care Center (ACC). The SCPH will house faculty and staff offices, research areas, and training labs for the Robert Stempel College of Public Health and Social Work. The complex will serve to consolidate the Florida Department of Health's (FDOH) administrative and public health units, including some outpatient clinics and clinical research labs facilitating efficient and effective provision of state-of-the-art diagnostic and laboratory services. The College of Medicine's ACC will include family medicine and primary care, sports medicine, an imaging center, and administrative and support spaces.

The center will solidify FIUs commitment to sustainability and its leadership position within the south-east region in developing new strategies for built environments that enhance healing, promote health, and create responsible environments that can help educate the community.

1   *View from southwest*

2   *Interior view of main courtyard*

Universidade Agostinho Neto

Luanda, Angola

Design completion: 2008
Estimated construction completion: 2010 (Phase I)
Client: Ministry of Education and Culture
Area: 330,000 square feet

This masterplan and design for a new national university on the outskirts of Luanda, Angola, is an opportunity arising from the cessation of the country's decades-long civil war and the consequent ability to direct its resources to education and renewal. The masterplan for a 5000-acre campus for 17,000 students consists of a core of academic buildings with research and residential buildings to the south and north respectively. Phase I, currently under construction, includes four classroom building housing the chemistry, mathematics, physics, and computer sciences faculties, and the central library and plaza. A refectory, student union, and conference center are also included. The entire campus should be completed over the next 10 to 15 years.

The guiding principle of the masterplan is low-maintenance sustainable urbanism. Development is concentrated on the semi-arid rolling site, leaving as much of the existing vegetation and river washes as possible untouched. The ring road is conceived as a pure circle, distorted into an ellipse to fit between the washes. Within the ellipse, which differentiates natural landscape from man-made pedestrian streets, quadrangles pinwheel from the central plaza. The orientation of the man-made grid is approximately 19 degrees east of the north–south axis, a compromise between the ideal solar orientation and the need to be perpendicular to the prevailing southwest breezes. Landscaping within the site channels the wind to maximize natural ventilation and cooling.

Natural cooling also drives individual building locations and the design of the building envelope. A single undulating roof draws breezes into the shaded courtyards and from there through open-air corridors and classroom spaces. The classroom buildings are single-loaded to facilitate ventilation. The engineered roof shading system of galvanized steel is calibrated to minimize solar gain and act as an airfoil to promote cross-ventilation through the bars by maximizing pressure differentiation. Exterior circulation paths and courtyards are shaded by the same roof system.

The spatial organization is also a response to the clients' desire for a democratic aesthetic. The pinwheel organization places various colleges equidistant from the academic core where the library, the tallest building on campus, dominates the central space and arrival place.

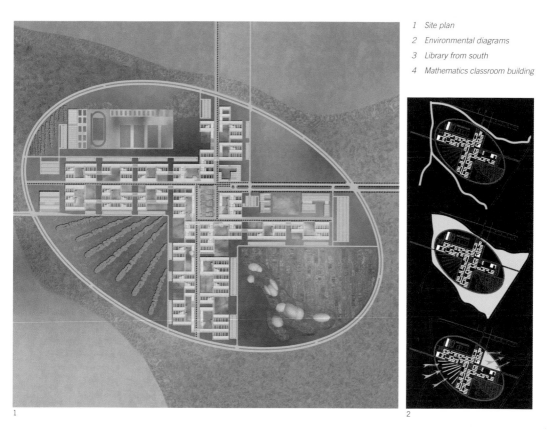

1 Site plan
2 Environmental diagrams
3 Library from south
4 Mathematics classroom building

Xi'an Jiaotong Liverpool University Integrated Science Building

Suzhou, People's Republic of China

Design completion: 2010
Client: Xi'an Jiaotong Liverpool University
Area: 450,000 square feet

Xi'an Jiaotong Liverpool University is a partnership between Xi'an Jiaotong University and the University of Liverpool in the United Kingdom. Enriching a long relationship with China, the University of Liverpool aims to encourage education abroad through this collaboration.

The design of this campus reflects the various cultural and environmental influences through strong signature characteristics. It is divided into three zones that offer three distinct campus environments: an academic village, an administrative center with shared resources, and a contemplative nature garden that incorporates features of traditional Chinese water gardens. Providing a centrally located natural space for the life of the campus, the nature garden links together an existing academic building, library, student activities center, and international dorm. The academic village concentrates classroom, faculty, office, and laboratory spaces in a manner that enhances opportunities for productive interactions among all building occupants.

The first phase of the master plan is Academic Building #2, a five-story building consisting of four separate wings connected by a second-level circulation loop. In each wing, a landscape fashioned to integrate two-story lecture halls supports and creates the form for the upper levels. Unique academic courtyards with water features provide additional access to nature. At the third level, the green roofs of the lecture halls provide additional exterior informal learning spaces. Multiple points of access and circulation through a series of raised interior and exterior environments facilitate movement through the building and increase the amount of spontaneous interaction between students, faculty, and staff, adding a dimension of urbanity and unexpectedness to the academic experience.

In addition to green roofs, the campus incorporates additional sustainable features. The design of Academic Building #2 maximizes access to natural light with a glass façade and reduces energy use with sunshades and shaded pedestrian areas. Stormwater is also conserved through pond systems that collect water runoff. Green spaces abound, giving occupants and visitors rich and varied moments of dialogue between the built and natural learning environments.

1   *View looking northeast*

2   *Aerial view*

3   *Campus view*

1

2

3

Dallas International School

Dallas, Texas, USA

Design completion: 2009
Estimated construction completion: 2011
Client: Dallas International School
Area: 140,000 square feet

Dallas International School's core principles rely fundamentally on academic strength in a multi-cultural environment. The school's new campus will serve a maximum of 950 students between the ages of 3 and 18. The design includes academic spaces to support classroom instruction in the sciences, art, music, and technology, as well as specialized spaces for language instruction. In phase I, spaces for the College (middle school) and Lycee (high school) students will be constructed, along with many of the shared spaces such as the media center, cafeteria, and gym. Most of the site work will also be finalized, including parking and vehicle circulation routes. In phase II, further expansion will take place for the school's Maternelle (pre-school) and Elementaire (elementary) students who will join the campus in their permanent location. The competition soccer field at the north end of the site will also be completed.

The building's layout nurtures social and academic development in a safe and secure environment, while introducing a series of program-specific courtyards designed to foster social interaction, outdoor learning, and provide each grade with their own academic identity. These courtyards are the "living rooms" of the school, where everyone meets. They are where all the memorable school rituals take place. The courtyards are the "real" classrooms where everyone learns to live, work, and play together, and where the school's most important values are imparted to students.

The buildings and the enclosed classrooms are therefore merely the frames, the physical walls that define the courtyards. These frames are relentlessly, almost without concession, planned to be running east–west to promote energy efficiency and protect the buildings from the harsh Texas sun while giving all the classrooms ample natural daylight.

The parallel east–west building configuration also provides the school with flexibility. The buildings simply get longer or shorter when the school needs more or fewer classrooms. Unlike closed-loop configurations, this linear configuration ensures the building is never "landlocked" for future expansion or modification.

The front entrance of the school is graced with a pair of parallel sun-hoods, a heroic cantilever welcoming visitors to Texas and to the school, the home of the international school community.

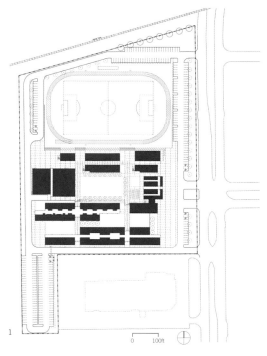

1   Site plan

2   East elevation highlighting
    entry and sun-hoods

3   North elevation view from
    soccer field highlighting
    classroom bar

4   Outdoor classroom circulation

Shanghai High School International Division

Shanghai, People's Republic of China

Design completion: 2010
Estimated construction completion: 2014
Client: Shanghai High School
Area: 192,000 square feet

School architecture is neither purely art nor science, but a combination of both in the service of the fundamental human desire to learn. The site chosen places the school alongside the Chuanyang River. Like the water, the students will move forward in varying directions but will always continue to change and grow.

The students who will attend this school will walk on paths parallel to the river, converging and blending as they flow between the classroom branches. The three floors of classrooms face south and allow the maximum amount of sunlight into the building. The classrooms will be shaded by a terracotta screen that will filter the direct sunlight, just as Chinese window screens have done for centuries. A rain garden will rest between the two wings of classrooms, collecting rainwater from the roofs of the buildings and slowly filtering it back through the natural landscape.

The main entry will be an area filled with dappled natural light during the day. The ramp and stairs of the main entry will be made of stone and will be the cornerstone of the solid foundation of the school. Located directly adjacent to the main entry, the centralized administrative functions will be highly visible and accessible to visitors, while at the same time keeping the school safe and secure. These administrative offices will have views of a landscaped and light-filled outdoor courtyard.

The overall building planning carefully groups the larger shared functions (such as the canteen and athletic areas) together, allowing this portion of the school to be open and available after normal school hours and on weekends. The second level gymnasium is accessible from a dedicated ground-floor lobby and overlooks the track and field area, keeping all athletic functions on the western side of the site. To increase the efficiency of the site, several athletic courts are located on the roof of the athletic wing.

The library/media center is the philosophical and physical heart of the school. Located on the second floor at the crossroad of all of the major building wings, the library is directly between the two academic wings. The library will have ample natural light from a raised sloping roof that will act as a glowing beacon and access point to an outdoor garden formed by the two academic wings.

1 Aerial view from southwest

2 View of main entry plaza

3 Site plan

4 View from east

Beirut Hotel and Residences

Beirut, Lebanon

Design completion: 2008
Estimated construction completion: 2015
Client: Confidential
Area: 646,000 square feet

This project comprises a five-star, 250-key hotel and 31 branded condominiums set across a rocky bluff at the edge of the sea. A 75-foot wall of limestone separates the property from the water across a vehicular boulevard. The entire sea edge is a water-carved landscape that reveals the city's geology in the limestone strata.

The temperate seaside climate supports significant outdoor activity; the Beirut Hotel and Residences explores this environment through the architecture of a beach-less resort on the water's edge that nonetheless participates in a lifestyle of leisure and sun. A 3-meter "collar" of outdoor space rings every hotel and residential floor outside the glazed weather enclosure of the dwelling units. This space is envisioned as a series of private beach cabanas that visually connect to the water. The cabanas are sheathed in a lattice of wood slats under which oversized curtained daybeds sit on a rough ground of sand-faced cast-in-place concrete.

The outer layer of the cabanas is the visual image of the building; here, a complex system of sliding, perforated cast-metal panels filter the strong sunlight and afford privacy to the cabana occupants when desired. The entire façade is sheathed in this semi-transparent skin, which throughout the day is transformed by the occupants' act of opening and closing each private cabana. The hotel and residences' maintenance program wipes the façade clean twice daily by closing the panels, during late-morning and early-evening room servicing, recording and re-writing the daily cycle of occupancy.

Built atop the limestone strata, the dwelling units are stacked vertically in a way that heightens the distinction between layers of individual residences, without imposing an artificial alignment that visually absorbs the program into a single Euclidian form.

1   *Building overview at dusk*

2   *Detail of façade screen wall*

3   *Materials study for screen wall*

4   *Personal spa (typical hotel bathroom)*

5   *Plan of typical king leisure suite*

6   *Study model*

1

2

3

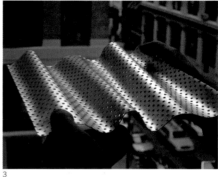

4

5

6

CP-70 (High-Rise Competition)

Abu Dhabi, United Arab Emirates

Design completion: 2008
Client: Confidential
Area: 4.7 million square feet

The competition brief outlined a mixed-use commercial high-rise building for a prominent location on the Abu Dhabi Corniche, the grand pedestrian and vehicular boulevard fronting the Persian Gulf. The client asked Perkins+Will to present five design alternatives and develop a program of approximately 4.7 million square feet composed of office, hotel, banquet hall, retail, and parking facilities, with a maximum height restriction of 980 feet.

The design team looked to typological and sustainable strategies as the foundation of design. The history of the development of the "skyscraper" reads like a provisional technical manual, evolving from masonry bearing wall structures to the steel frame construction that could more appropriately respond to market-driven requirements such as more building area (through additional floors), more efficient floor plans, and greater amounts of natural light. Responding to qualitative contemporary needs, this competition entry challenged issues such as human scale, environmental indifference, floor plate inefficiency, and speed of construction.

The sequence of five design proposals began with the most conventional organization and evolved toward more speculative designs that suggested creative, relevant solutions while adhering to the contemporary expectations for place making and visual intrigue. The final proposal separated the tower into four strands of differing heights. The strands are separate and flared at the lower levels and combine at the upper levels to form the primary shaft of the tower. Through the form and organization of the building it creates a civic, iconic urban presence, allows for distinct entry points for each program type, and offers floor plate sizing that can be adjusted even during the construction process to meet market demand.

The team found that as the aspirations for skyscrapers continue to evolve, the process, too, must find strategies that can operate within a contextual vacuum with very deliberate, built-in adaptability. Beyond singular attributes of image-making or tallest building, the new model can allow for hybrid programs, market volatility, site adaptability, and human-centric considerations. These aspects of the final product speak more to the spirit of the place and become a memorable part of its city by expanding the limits of a specific building typology.

1 View southwest with Persian Gulf beyond

1

Heping Residential Development
Tianjin, People's Republic of China

Design completion: 2004
Estimated construction completion: 2010
Client: Tianjin Tianchuang Real Estate Co., Ltd.
Area: 1.2 million square feet

This development is a collection of six 33-story residential buildings
with varying floor plates and unit designs that respond to both middle
and upper income brackets.

The residential tower designs, while not identical, employ a similar
architectural vocabulary. They are site-cast concrete buildings with glass
infill between each floor level. The major south and north elevations
make use of an architectural parti that is a series of two-story "folded
plains" that emerge from the towers' floor plates and project beyond
the façade to create a series of balconies along the entire façade of the
building. These alternating folds create a two-story articulation that is
punctuated by smaller projecting balconies on the intermediate floors.
Screen elements are used as required to mask the location and
projections of external air conditioning units and large-scale louver
elements are used to unify the vertical transportations cores. The tops
of the buildings culminate in the wrapping of the "folding plain" that
climbs the façades and ultimately conceals the mechanical and service
penthouses of the buildings. This architectural vocabulary gives each
building an iconic stance that collectively works to create a new design
aesthetic for the Heping neighborhood.

The development's "central park" is a series of articulating ribbons
and folded plains that grow from the lawn at the park's west end
and culminate as the roofs of the three pavilions that comprise the
Community Building on the site's east end. The park is planted with
a combination of lawn and sedums that reinforce through their
planting scheme the articulating ribbons that are the focus of this
dynamic landscape.

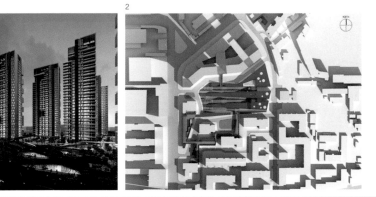

1 View from north
2 Site plan
3 Park from west

3

Kempinski Hotel and Residences SailTower

Jeddah, Saudi Arabia

Design completion: 2009
Estimated construction completion: 2014
Client: Al-Issa Real Estate Development Company
Area: 680,000 square feet

Inspired by its prominent location directly on the Red Sea, this project explores the concept of the "architectural sail" as a multifunctional architectonic element that responds to the essential influences of program, site, and climate to create a unique expression of texture and light.

The project, situated along the Corniche in Jeddah, marks the transition between the desert landscape and the Red Sea, and extends the growth of waterfront development advancing north from the old city center. The recent growth of Jeddah as a resort destination has raised the matter of how to create successful hospitality environments that address both climatic and cultural issues.

The brief calls for a mixture of luxury hotel functions, serviced apartments, and condominiums, with below-grade parking for 600 cars. The client requested that the tower be as tall as zoning permitted. The building is a simple, slender rectangle, oriented along the east–west axis to optimize solar exposure, shade the entrance court to the north, and maximize views to the water. Major program elements are organized as a continuous ribbon from below grade to the penthouse, becoming more private as they rise. Correspondingly, balcony size increases with height to create outdoor rooms at the upper residential levels.

This gradual deepening of exterior space and rotation of the architectural sails to open to the view creates a dramatic pattern and texture for the skin of the building while giving privacy between adjacent rooms, orienting views to the water, and limiting the negative effects of sun and wind. Because the panels rotate to perpendicular at the top of the building where the balconies are deepest, the building transforms from an expression that is primarily surface at its base to one that is primarily void as the enclosure dematerializes with height. The sails in turn become sources of light in the evening, with integrated LED fixtures providing a soft glow that can be programmed to create a dynamic, flowing array throughout the entire surface of the building. This approach, based on innovative tectonics rather than formal gesture, results in a unique architectural expression with a clear sense of place and identity.

1   *View looking southeast*

2   *Residential interior*

3   *Lobby*

4   *Pool deck*

1

2

3

4

Kempinski Hotel and Residences SailTower   309

Campus for Research Excellence and Technological Enterprise

Singapore

Design completion: 2009
Estimated construction completion: 2011
Client: National Research Foundation
Area: 800,000 square feet

The Campus for Research Excellence and Technological Enterprise (CREATE) is the gateway to the National University of Singapore's eastward campus expansion. It is a unique multi-national, multi-disciplinary research enterprise with the primary mission of stimulating innovation, discovery, and entrepreneurship through the interaction and collaboration of scientists and engineers.

The CREATE campus is composed of three mid-rise buildings interlaced with landscape and a high-rise tower sharing a covered pedestrian town center. The tower engages a podium that houses student amenities at grade and CREATE's headquarter facilities at level two. CREATE's long, column-free, unusually narrow building modules allow daylight to penetrate and naturally illuminate the interior spaces, significantly reducing energy consumption. Views to the landscaped gardens are abundant, enhancing the research environment. The tower, designed on the same narrow module, features a series of three-story vertical sky gardens accessible from the upper levels.

The design pioneers advanced environmental sustainability and energy-efficient technologies. The buildings are oriented on the east–west axis for optimal solar control and to engage and collect natural flow of water from the hills to the east. Integral sustainable features include rainwater harvesting from the canopies and plaza areas, stored and used to fulfill basic water requirements; roof and awning-mounted photovoltaic panels, and green roofs to reduce stormwater runoff and minimize interior heat gain. The landscape design, a restorative garden setting for flora and fauna, was inspired by Singapore's famous Botanical Gardens.

Interaction beyond the lab is possible through a rich and diverse sequence of shared and social spaces, that weave form, space, and light into places for collaboration and collision, disruptive innovation, and contemplative solitude, essential ingredients of a productive research environment. Set in a garden, CREATE will be a vibrant place, a dense urban organism where the ecosystem, environmental art, and scientific discovery meet in a union of opposites: a tower in the garden, science in the rainforest.

Opposite   Aerial of campus from south

Oklahoma Medical Research Foundation Research Tower

Oklahoma City, Oklahoma, USA

Design completion: 2009
Estimated construction completion: 2010
Client: Oklahoma Medical Research Foundation
Area: 195,000 square feet

The Oklahoma Medical Research Foundation (OMRF) is a non-profit biomedical investigative medical research entity, performing mainly molecular-level research into diseases including Alzheimer's, lupus, cancer, and cardiovascular disease.

The new research tower sits at the heart of the foundation's campus, providing state-of-the-art research facilities, linking the existing buildings together, and adding an iconic, forward-looking image for the city's skyline. The ground floor houses shared core laboratories including imaging and a vivarium with procedural support labs. The main level houses a new research clinic and support amenities to serve the entire campus. The upper floors have eight principal investigators on each floor, allowing the building to accommodate a minimum of 34 new principal investigators that will boost OMRF employment to more than 800 people when the building is fully occupied.

Connected by a bridge to the existing building to the north, a two-story transparent lobby sits atop an elevated base containing research support spaces. To the south, the base steps down in a series of planted terraces and stairways. Excess water from the building's mechanical system is channeled into a pool that surrounds the lobby and outdoor event spaces then cascades down a waterfall before being stored in an underground cistern for irrigation.

Above the lobby, the main mass of the building is cut by four deep slots that bring light and views deep into the central core of the building and divide the mass into four distinct blocks. Each block, in turn, shifts vertically to accommodate the program above and below them. The resulting "pinwheel" plan provides a unique character and identity to the individual research labs.

Precast concrete bands wrap each block, providing shading to the east and west façades and lifting up at the northeast and southwest blocks to support and channel wind to 24 rooftop turbines. These turbines and photovoltaic panels will serve as alternative energy sources and will generate approximately 10 percent of the energy for the building. At the northwest corner, a rooftop garden provides views of the state capitol and the turbines directly overhead.

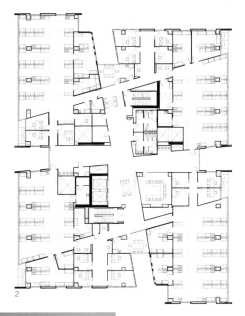

1 Main entry view with wind turbines

2 Typical research floor plan

3 West view

4 East view

ENDMATTER

Project Credits

LEGACY

100 North Riverside

Client: Orix Ral Estate Equities
Design Principal: Ralph E. Johnson
Managing Principal: James C. Allen
Project Manager: Charles Anderson
Senior Designer: August Battaglia
Project Designer: Mark Romack
Project Team: Laura Alberga, Paul Hagle, Mike Hoffman, Jerry Johnson, John Karabatsos, Carlos Parilla, Stuart Royalty, Eric Spielman, Steven Ward, Phil Zinny
Image Credits: Nick Merrick of Hedrich Blessing (1–2)

Crate & Barrel Corporate Headquarters

Client: Crate & Barrel
Design Principal: Ralph E. Johnson
Managing Principals: G. William Doerge, Terrence M. Owens
Project Manager: Michael Palmer
Project Designer: Hans Thummel
Project Team: John Andrea, Richard Gnat, Terri Johnson, Jennifer Pedtke, Alexandra Schabel
Image Credits: Nick Merrick of Hedrich Blessing (1–3)

Don Imus-WFAN Pediatric Center, Hackensack Medical Center

Client: Hackensack Medical Center
Design Principal: Audrey Matlock
Managing Principal: Joseph Shein
Planning Principal: Donald Blair
Project Manager: David Wilklow
Senior Designers: Tom Love, Lisa Gould
Project Designers: Georgine Ilesco, David Whitaker
Project Team: Lou Bauko, Pat Daly, Mimi Garza, James Huey, Jose Madrigal, Richard Mariano, Raphael Neja, Bennett Reed, KK Tey, Joanne Violante
Image Credits: Esto Photographics, Inc. (1–4)

International School of Beijing

Client: International School of Beijing
Associate Architect: Beijing Institute of Architectural Design + Research
Design Principal: Lisa Gould
Managing Principal: Ray Bordwell
Project Managers: Amy Yurko, Charles Alexander
Project Designer: Ron Vitale
Project Architects: David Cerruti, Peter Brown
Project Team: Mark Bastian, Marina deConciliis, John Gerney, Benjamin Gilmartin, Peggy Hoffman, David Powell, Michael Poynton, Kevin Rice, Stephen Sharlach
Image Credits: Hans Schlupp (1–4)

McDonnell Pediatric and Cancer Research Building

Client: Washington University School of Medicine
Associate Architect: Mackey Michell Associates /GPR Planners
    Collaborative Inc. (Lab Planners)
Design Principal: Ralph E. Johnson
Managing Principal: John Nunemaker
Project Manager: Paul Clinch
Senior Designers: William Schmalz, Geoffrey Brooksher
Project Designer: Jerry Johnson
Project Team: Scott Cyphers, Thomas Czyzyk, David Dunn,
    Bryan Schabel, Elias Vavaroutsos, James Vira
Image Credits: James Steinkamp (1–3)

Neuroscience Research Building

Client: University of California, Los Angeles (UCLA)
Lab Planners: GPR Planners Collaborative Inc.
Design Principal: Ralph E. Johnson
Technical Principal: Fred Afshari
Project Manager: Paul Clinch
Senior Designer: Louis Raia
Project Architects: Thomas Braham, David Powell
Project Team: Nathalie Belanger, Jack Bransfield, Raymond Coleman,
    Philip Hung, Monica Oller, Bryan Schabel
Image Credits: James Steinkamp (1–2, 4)

Orland Park Village Center

Client: Village of Orland Park, Illinois
Design Principal: Ralph E. Johnson
Managing Principal: Terrence M. Owens
Project Manager: Charles Anderson
Project Designer: August Battaglia
Project Team: Pamela Kurz, Carlos Parilla, Robin Randall, Carolyn Smith,
    Steven Ward, George Witaszek
Image Credits: Nick Merrick for Hedrich Blessing (1, 3)

Peggy Notebaert Nature Center

Client: Chicago Academy of Sciences
Exhibit Design: Lee H. Skolnick Architecture + Design Partnership
Design Principal: Ralph E. Johnson
Project Director: Terrence M. Owens
Senior Designer: Thomas Mozina
Project Architect: Michael Poynton
Project Team: Michael Bowers, Geoffrey Brooksher, Nicola Casciato,
    David Dunn, Jerry Johnson, Jeff Olson, David Poorman, Tyler Shyrer,
    Elias Vavroutsos
Image Credits: James Steinkamp (1–3)

Perry Community Educational Village

Client: Perry Local School District
Associate Architect: Burgess & Niple, Ltd
Managing Principal: Ralph E. Johnson
Project Director: Raymond Bordwell
Project Manager: James Toya
Project Designers: August Battaglia, James Woods
Technical Coordinators: James Nowak, William Schamlz
Project Team: Gregory Bennett, Jerry Johnson, Mike Palmer,
    Carlos Parilla, Robin Randall, Celeste Robbins, Robert Ruggles,
    Eric Spielman, Randy Takahashi
Image Credits: Nick Merrick for Hedrich Blessing (1–2)

Temple Hoyne Buell Hall

Client: University of Illinois, Urbana-Champaign /Capital Development
    Board
Design Principal: Ralph E. Johnson
Managing Principal: John Nunemaker
Project Manager: Scott Reed
Project Designer: Vojo Narancic
Technical Coordinator: Robert Gross
Project Team: Dean Huspen, Gary Jaeger, Steve Turckes, Thomas Vecchio
Image Credits: Nick Merrick for Hedrich Blessing (1–3)

Terminal 5, O'Hare International Airport

Client: City of Chicago, Department of Aviation
Associate Architects: Heard & Associates, Ltd./Consoer Townsend
  & Associates
Design Principal: Ralph E. Johnson
Managing Principal: James M. Stevenson
Project Manager: James E. Economos
Senior Designer: August Battaglia
Project Designer: Elizabeth Fakatselis
Project Planner: Mark Romack
Project Team: Fred Afshari, Susan Barnes, Steve Bogay, Davor Engle,
  Mike Gillaspie, Dina Griffin, Doug Grimm, Paul Hagle, Mark Jolicoeur,
  Thomas Kamis, Henry Lee, Paul Pettigrew, Jon Pohl, Michael Poynton,
  Joseph Pullara, Larry Robertson, Robert Ruggles, Billy Tindel,
  Bernie Wotek, Phil Zinny
Image Credits: Nick Merrick for Hedrich Blessing (1–2)

Tribune Interactive

Client: Chicago Tribune
Design Principal: Ralph E. Johnson
Managing Principal: James Prendergast
Project Manager: Frank Pettinati
Project Designer: Jason Rosenblatt
Project Architect: William Berger
Project Team: Nathalie Belanger, Lindsay Steinacher
Image Credits: Steve Hall for Hedrich Blessing (1–2, 4)

Troy High School

Client: Troy Public Schools
Design Principal: Ralph E. Johnson
Managing Principal: C. William Brubaker
Project Manager: James Toya
Project Designer: John Arzarian, Jr.
Project Team: Geoffrey Brooksher, Susan Emmons, Elizabeth Fakatselis,
  Mike Hoffman, Robin Randall, Eric Spielman, George Witaszek
Image Credits: Nick Merrick for Hedrich Blessing (2–4)

W.W. Grainger, Inc. Headquarters

Client: W.W. Grainger, Inc.
Interior Architect: The Environments Group
Design Principal: David Hansen
Managing Principal: Terrence M. Owens
Senior Designers: Michael Henthorn, Randy Guillot
Senior Technical Assistant: Jim Novak
Project Architects: John Bowers, Hans Thummel, Marty Jurasek
Project Team: Todd Baisch, Michelle Fisher, Peggy Hoffman, David Powell
Image Credits: Steve Hall for Hedrich Blessing (1–4)

CURRENT

235 Van Buren

Client: CMK Development Corporation
Design Principal: Ralph E. Johnson
Managing Principal: Bridget Lesniak
Project Designer: Bryan Schabel
Project Architects: Robert Neper, Greg Tamborino
Project Team: Ricardo Escutia, Connie Perry, Alissa Piere, Tara Rejniak, Chris Wolf
Image Credits: James Steinkamp (1–3, 6–7)

Arizona State University, Interdisciplinary Science & Technology Building I

Client: Arizona State University
Lab Planners: GPR Planners Collaborative Inc.
Design Principal: Ralph E. Johnson
Managing Principal: Michael Smith
Project Manager: John Becker
Project Designers: Bryan Schabel, Cengiz Yetken
Project Architect: Lewis Wood
Project Team: Scott Allen, Bill Berger, Yong Cai, Mary Guerrero, Jeff Olson, Cesar Pineda, Michele Sainte-Starbuck, Lynette Tedder, Mariah Walters
Image Credits: James Steinkamp (1, 3–7)

Arts & Social Sciences Complex

Client: Simon Fraser University
Design Principals: Peter Busby, David Dove
Managing Principal: David Dove
Project Manager: Susan Ockwell
Project Team: Benn Duffell, Brian Gasmena, Bob Greig, Daniel Roberts
Image Credits: Enrico Dagostini (1), Nic Lehoux (2, 4–5)

Atrisco Heritage Academy

Client: Albuquerque Public Schools
Associate Architect: Fanning Bard Tatum Architects AIA, Ltd.
Managing Principal: Wendell Vaughn
Interior Design Principal: Jo Carmen
Project Manager: Eric Brossy de Dios
Senior Interior Designer: Angela Kunz
Senior Project Architect: Victor Garcia
Project Designers: Wendell Vaughn, Marcelo Igonda
Project Architect: Ann Knudsen
Project Team: Olga Bespalova, Patrick Glenn, Cheryl Jacobs, Brian Knight, Charlene Martin, Keven Mereness, Patrick Morey, Carlos Ramirez, Ashley Stoner
Image Credits: New York Focus (1, 4, 6), Fanning Bard Tatum Architects (1, 5), Marcelo Igonda (7)

August Wilson Center for African American Culture

Client: August Wilson Center for African American Culture
Design Principal: Allison Williams
Branded Environments Design Principal: Eva L. Maddox
Managing Principal: Allison Williams
Brand Account Manager: J.D. McKibben
Project Managers: Marc Arnold, Gretchen Mokry
Project Team: Sally Curtis, Patrick Grzybek, Gregory Lehman, James Mallery, Smita Modi, Phillip Ohingo, Zeljko Pavlovic, Hyuek Rhee, Patrick Riddle, Jessica Sager, Mayank Singh, Stanley Vistica, Christian Wopperer
Image Credits: James Steinkamp (1–3, 5)

Bank of America Corporate Center (Workplace Prototype)

Client: Bank of America
Design Principal: Eva L. Maddox
Client Account Manager: John Morris
Brand Platform Development: Eileen E. Jones
Planning + Strategy: Janice Barnes
Workplace Innovation: Rod Vickroy
Interior Architecture: Gardner Vass
Interior Design: Laura Smith, Remiko Kitazawa, Rebecca Krupp
LEED & Sustainability: Anne Jackson
Environmental Graphics: Deborah Beckett
Signage & Wayfinding: Samar Hechaime, Chris Mueller
Flythrough Rendering: Mikhail Margulis
Image Credits: Steve Hall (1–2, 5–7)

Blythewood High School

Client: Richland School District Two
Design Principal: Jerry Johnson
Managing Principal: Steven Turckes
Programming Principal: Ray Bordwell
Project Designer: Yan Ding
Project Architects: Hans Thummel, Aimee Eckmann
Project Team: Peter Brown, Yan Ding
Image Credits: James Steinkamp (1, 3, 5–6), The Southern Management Group (2)

Brentwood Town Center Station

Client: Rapid Transit Project Office
Design Principal: Peter Busby
Managing Principal: Martin Nielsen
Project Manager: Teryl Mullock
Project Team: Brian Billingsley, Marco Bonaventura, Scott Edwards, Richard Peck, Soren Schou, Adam Slawinski
Image Credits: Nic Lehoux (1–2, 5–8)

CDC National Center for Environmental Health Building 110

Client: Centers for Disease Control and Prevention
Design Principals: Manuel Cadrecha, Amy Sickeler
Managing Principal: Dan Watch
Project Manager: Bertrand Piquet
Project Designer: David Rogers
Senior Planner: Deepa Tolat
Interior Project Architect: Grace Paul
Project Architects: Mark Rahe, Floyd Cline
Project Team: Stuart Aynsley, Michael Hodge, John Mlade, Don Reynolds, Nicole Sheffield, Paula Vaughan
Image Credits: Nick Merrick for Hedrich Blessing (1–5)

Center for Urban Waters

Client: National Development Council
Managing Principal: Kay Kornovich
Planning Principal: Kay Kornovich
Project Manager: Daniel Seng
Project Designer: Tony DeEulio
Project Architect: Tony DeEulio
Project Team: Shannon Brown, Jason Chiu, Devin Kleiner
Image Credits: Benjamin Benschneider (1, 4–6)

Central Middle School

Client: Bartholomew Consolidated School Corporation
Associate Architect: CSO
Design Principal: Ralph E. Johnson
Managing Principal: Steve Turckes
Project Manager: Michael Palmer
Project Designer: Bryan Schabel
Project Architect: Mark Walsh
Project Team: Shannon Gedey, Eileen Pedersen, Bryce Tolene
Image Credits: James Steinkamp (1–3, 5–7), Greg Murphy (4)

Chervon International Trading Company

Client: Chervon Group
Associate Architect: Nanjing Design Institute, People's Republic of China
Design Principal: Ralph E. Johnson
Managing Principal: G. William Doerge
Project Manager: William Berger
Project Designer: Thomas Demetrion
Project Architect: Marius Ronnett
Project Team: Kimberly Creswell, Yan Ding, Hahn Joh, Jason Rosenblatt, Alex Therien, Khai Toh
Image Credits: James Steinkamp (1, 4–7), Wu Pei Jun, Chun Shang Advertising and Arts Co., Ltd. (3)

Clark County Elementary School Prototype

Client: Clark County School District
Associate Architect: JMA Architecture
Design Principal: Nick Seierup
Managing Principal: Wendell Vaughn
Project Manager: Eric Brossy de Dios
Project Architect: Tinka Rogic
Project Team: Guy Horton, James Kerrigan, Angela Kunz, Ashley Stoner
Image Credits: Perkins+Will

Computer Sciences Building

Client: York University
Design Principal: Peter Busby
Project Manager: Mike McColl
Project Team: Veronica Gillies, Susan Ockwell, Alfred Waugh
Associated Architectural Team: Van Nostrand DiCastry Architects
Image Credits: Steven Evans (1–2, 5–9)

Confidential Financial Services Client

Client: Confidential
Design Principals: Eileen Jones, Joan Blumenfeld
Managing Principal: Lisa Pool
Workplace Consulting Principal: Paul Eagle
Production/Coordination Principal: John Fuller
Project Director: Sonya Dufner
Project Team: Patrick Grzybek, Victor Kung, Rachel Robinson, Leonard Temko, Simon Trude
Image Credits: Steve Hall for Hedrich Blessing (2, 4–5)

Contemporaine

Client: CMK Development Corporation
Design Principal: Ralph E. Johnson
Technical Principal: Fred Afshari
Project Managers: Nicol Chervenak, Dave Gutierrez
Project Designer: Bryan Schabel
Project Architect: Marius Ronnett
Project Team: Curt Behnke, Nicolette Brandstedt, Raymond Coleman, Steve Santucci, Cengiz Yetken
Image Credits: James Steinkamp (1–4, 6–8)

Darden Restaurants Corporate Headquarters Building

Client: Darden Restaurants
Design Principals: Manuel Cadrecha, Joyce Fownes, Eileen Jones,
  Leo Alvarez
Managing Principal: Donald Reynolds
Project Designers: Bruce McEvoy, Eric Lane
Project Architect: Thomas Pederson
Interior Architect: Kim Chamness
Interior Project Designer: Christy Cain
Project Team: Justin Cooper, Christian Cotter, Ryan Dagley,
  Erinn Dornaus, Brian Erlinder, Rick Harrison, Cathy Jensen,
  Meena Krenek, Veronica Logsdon, Jahae Park Orr, Julia Phillips,
  Nancy Shea-Quigley, Alexander Stewart, Leonard Temko, Chris Wong,
  Ellen Young
On Site Construction Representative: Rick Harrison
Image Credits: Steve Hall for Hedrich Blessing (1–2, 4–5)

Dockside Green

Client: Dockside Green Ltd. Partnership (Vancity and Windmill West)
Design Principals: Peter Busby, Brian Wakelin, Jim Huffman
Managing Principal: Terry Williams, Robert Drew
Project Managers: Rod Maas
Project Team: Erik Berglund, Leo Chester, Paul Cowcher,
  Michael Driedger, Adam Fawkes, Chris Foyd, Peter Johannknecht,
  Tim Judge, David Kitazaki, Rod Maas, Samantha Patterson,
  Jeff Skinner, Adam Slawinski, Gerry Underhill, Kathy Wardle
Image Credits: Enrico Dagostini (2, 4, 6), Vince Klassen (3, 5)

Equal Employment Opportunity Commission (EEOC)

Client: Equal Employment Opportunity Commission (EEOC)
Design Principal: Michael Considine
Managing Principal: Michael Considine
Project Manager: Michael Considine
Senior Designer: Tamara Cavin
Project Designer: David Cordell
Project Team: Marian Danowski, Thomas Gregory
Image Credits: Max Mackenzie (1–3, 5)

Great River Energy Headquarters

Client: Great River Energy
Design Principal: David Dimond
Project Manager: Gerald Voermans
Project Designer: Tony Layne
Project Architect: Douglas Pierce
Project Team: Thomas Beck, Jim Foran, Michelle Hammer,
  Meredith Hayes-Gordon, Ed Heinen, David Koenen, David Little,
  Kathryn Martenson, Russell Philstrom, Lisa Pool, Dennis Sachs,
  Jon Wollak
Image Credits: Lucie Marusin (1), Paul Crosby (2, 4), Don Wong (3)

Haworth Showrooms

Client: Haworth, Inc.
Global Showroom Design Leadership 2004–2009
Managing Principal: Eva L. Maddox (2004–09)
Brand Strategy Principal: Eileen Jones (2004–09)
Workplace Innovation Associate Principal: Rod Vickroy (2004–06)
Interiors Associate Principal: Frank Pettinati (2004–05)
Interior Design Directors: Michael McCarthy (2005), Rod Vickroy (2006–07)
Creative Directors: Simon Trude (2007), Gerardo Fitz-Gibbon (2008–09)
Technical Coordinator: Patrick Grzybek (2004–2009)
Project Managers: Frank Pettinati (2005) Dawn Tuttle (2005–2007) Leonard Temko (2007–09), Geoff Miller (2007)
Project Architects: Ron Stelmarski (2004–2006), Victor Kung (2007)
Design Architect & Sustainability: Kim Chamness (2007)
Sustainable Design Advisor: Peter Busby (2007)
Design Principals: Brian Wakelin (2007), RK Stewart (2009)
Construction Administration: Peter Conrad (2009)
Image Credits: Steve Hall (1, 8), Nick Merrick (2–7), Marvin Rand (9)

Hector P. Garcia Middle School

Client: Dallas Independent School District
Managing Principal: Peter Brown
Project Manager: Patrick Glenn
Project Designers: Rusty Walker, Carol Cumbie
Project Architect: Patrick Glenn
Project Team: Andy Craigo, Justin Parscale, Mark Walsh
Image Credits: James Steinkamp (1–3, 5–7)

Interdisciplinary Life Sciences Building

Client: Texas A&M University System
Design Principal: Manuel Cadrecha
Managing Principal: Ed Cordes
Project Managers: Melissa Crispin, Mike Moreland
Senior Designer: David Rogers
Senior Planner: Dan Watch
Project Architects: Lea Anne Leatherwood, Jonathan Stokes
Project Team: Jason Chan, Alexander Clinton, Yves Gauthier, Jeff Kim, Steffi Kuehnlein, John Mlade, Catherine Nichols, Daniel Poehler, Diego Rozo, Stacey Wyman
Image Credits: Mark Trew (1–3, 5–7)

International Media Company

Client: Confidential
Design Principal: Joan Blumenfeld
Managing Principal: Joan Blumenfeld
Project Managers: Pamela Abalu, David Valenta
Project Designers: Steve South, Marco Marcellini, Luca Panhota
Project Team: Mi Young Lee, Katherine Lytle
Image Credits: Eduard Hueber for Arch Photo Inc. (1), Perkins+Will (2–3), Paúl Rivera for Arch Photo Inc.(4–6)

Intrepid Sea, Air & Space Museum

Client: Intrepid Sea, Air & Space Museum
Design Principals: Ralph E. Johnson, Eva L. Maddox
Account Manager: Leonard Temko
Project Architect: Ron Stelmarski
Project Team: Erinn Dornaus, Patrick Grzybek, Samar Hechaime, Lynette Klein, Kay Lee, Liz Mohl, Nicole Pallante, Ryan Roetker, Amanda Searfoss, Chris Wong, Ellen Young
Image Credits: Jon Miller for Hedrich Blessing (2–4, 7–8)

INVISTA Inc., Antron®
DuPont Antron® Resource Center

Client: E.I. DuPont De Nemours & Company
Design Principals: Eileen Jones, Eva Maddox
Project Team: Carly Cannell, Patrick Grzybek, Anna Kania, Melissa Kleve, Kay Lee, Ron Stelmarksi
Image Credits: Steve Hall for Hedrich Blessing (1, 3–6), Marco Lorenzetti (2)

Klaus Advanced Computing Building

Client: Georgia Institute of Technology
Design Principal: Manuel Cadrecha
Managing Principal: Gary McNay
Project Managers: Mark Rahe, Lee Percy
Project Designer: David Rogers
Project Architects: Floyd Cline, Kimberly Polkinhorn
Image Credits: Nick Merrick for Hedrich Blessing (1–2)

Labovitz School of Business and Economics

Client: University of Minnesota
Associate Architects: Stanius Johnson Architects (SJA)
Design Principal: Ralph E. Johnson
Managing Principal: Jeff Ziebarth
Project Manager: Eric Spielman
Project Designer: Thomas Mozina
Project Architect: Mark Walsh
Project Team: Jeff Hayner, Eileen Pederson, Bryce Tolene, Nathan Wilcox
Image Credits: James Steinkamp (1–5)

Los Angeles Police Department Rampart Station

Client: City of Los Angeles
Associate Architect: Roth + Sheppard Architects
Design Principal: Nick Seierup
Managing Principals: Mike Fejes, Gabrielle Bullock
Project Manager: Randy Larsen
Project Architect: Leigh Christy
Project Team: Teresa Cheung, Wilkie Choi, Wing Ho, Ryan Hollien
Image Credits: Michael Urbanek (1, 2, 4)

Materials Testing Laboratory

Client: City of Vancouver Engineering Services
Design Principal: Peter Busby
Project Manager: Mike McColl
Project Team: Stephan Chevalier, Dharini Thiruchittampalam
Image Credits: Martin Tessler (1–2, 4)

Mayo Clinic Replacement Hospital

Client: Mayo Clinic
Design Principals: Manuel Cadrecha, Carolyn BaRoss, Amy Sickeler
Managing Principal: David Johnson
Project Director: Don Shaffer
Project Designer: Bruce McEvoy
Senior Medical Planner: Gary Swords
Project Architects: Gary Justice, Don Reynolds
Project Team: Seth Benator, Diana Davis, Grace Paul, Nicole Sheffield
On Site Construction Representative: Rick Harrison
Image Credits: Nick Merrick for Hedrich Blessing (1, 3–5), Anton Grassl for Esto (6)

Miami Beach City Hall Annex

Client: City of Miami Beach
Design Principals: Pat Bosch, Marlene Liriano
Managing Principal: Jose Gelabert-Navia
Project Manager: Carlos Chiu
Project Architect: Julio Guillen
Project Team: George Betancourt, David Chamberlain, Lilia Gonzalez, Yong Lee, Camila Querasian
Image Credits: New York Focus (1, 4–5)

Nancy N. and J.C. Lewis Cancer and Research Pavilion

Client: St. Joseph's/Candler
Design Principal: James Smith
Managing Principals: David Johnson
Project Managers: Coleman Demoss, John Hogshead
Project Designers: David Rogers, David Sheehan
Project Architect: Thomas Pederson
Project Team: Andrew Crenshaw, William Price
Image Credits: Jim Roof (1, 5), Hedrich Blessing (2, 4, 6)

Nicola Valley Institute of Technology

Client: Nicola Valley Institute of Technology and University College of the Cariboo
Design Principal: Peter Busby
Managing Principal: Susan Gushe
Project Manager: Alfred Waugh
Project Team: Robert Drew, Veronica Gillies, Rod Maas, Soren Schou, Adam Slawinski, Brian Wakelin, Nathan Webster, Thomas Winkler
Image Credits: Nic Lehoux (1–3, 5–7)

Normand Maurice Building

Client: Public Works and Government Services Canada/Department of National Defense
Design Principal: Peter Busby
Managing Principal: Susan Gushe
Project Manager: Brian Wakelin
Project Team: Matt Galloway, Robin Glover, Michele Labrie, Rod Maas, Drahan Petrovic, Soren Schou, Adam Slawinski, Kathy Wardle
Associated Architectural Team: Beauchamp Bourbeau Arch ABCP Architecture & Urbanisme
Image Credits: Nic Lehoux (1–6); Marc Cramer (7)

North Campus Residence Hall

Client: Roger Williams University
Design Principal: John McDonald
Managing Principals: Timothy Marsters, Dana Anderson
Project Manager: David Damon
Project Architect: Andrew Grote
Project Team: Hye Yeon Cho, Bryony Darcy, Alan Estabrook, Fang-Chun Hsu, Kimberly Kelly, Christopher Lee
Image Credits: Anton Grassl/Esto (1, 9–10), Christian Phillips Photography (5–8)

NYU Stern School of Business Concourse Renovation Project

Client: New York University
Design Principals: Joan Blumenfeld, Eileen Jones
Managing Principal: Michael Kihn
Project Managers: Steven Wright, Anthony Alfieri, Kay Lee
Brand Strategist: Brian Weatherford
Project Designers: Rachel Robinson, Anne Kojima
Project Architect: Matt Cornett
Project Team: Patrick Grzybek, Brian Harris, Kyongju Kim, Smita Modi, Stephen Sharlach, Sam Stubblefield, Ellen Young, Jeff Ziebarth
Image Credits: Eduard Hueber, Arch Photo Inc. (1–5)

Ohlone College Newark Center for Health Sciences and Technology

Client: Ohlone Community College District
Managing Principal: Karen Cribbins-Kuklin
Project Manager: Susan Seastone
Lead Designer: Stevens Williams
Project Architect: Peter Conrad
Technical Coordinator: Nilda Marchan
Image Credits: Bob Canfield (1–6)

One Haworth Center

Client: Haworth, Inc.
Design Principals: Ralph E. Johnson, Eva L. Maddox
Managing Principal: Bridget Lesniak
Technical Principal: Bruce Toman
Brand Strategists: Eileen Jones, Brian Weatherford
Project Designers: Joachim Schuessler, Lou Raia
Project Manager: Al Kanter
Project Architect: Richard Schroeder, Mark Walsh
Architectural Project Team: Abul Abdullah, Alexis Anthony, CJ Armstrong, Gail Borthwick, Leon Chomicz, Bryce De Reynier, Krystian Gardula, Michelle Halle Stern, Michael Rafferty, Tara Rejniak, Argyro-Nikolet Scarlatis, Thomas Smith, Dennis St. John, Rusty Walker, James Wild, Richard Young
Branding Project Team: Ben Conely, Erinn Dornaus, Brian Erlinder, Amina Helstern, Anna Kania, Lynette Klein, J.D. McKibben, Ron Stelmarski, Leonard Temko, Simon Trude, Dawn Tuttle, Carl Washington
Interiors Project Team: Robert Cohoon, Laura Cook, Lisa Estep, Pat Grzybek, Cheri Jacobs, Rebecca Krupp, Hyun-Ju Oh, Rachel Payleitner, Frank Pettinati, Lisa Pool, Laura Smith, Rod Vickroy
Interiors Planning & Strategies Project Team: Janice Barnes, James Prendergast
Image Credits: Curt Clayton (1–2, 7) James Steinkamp (3–4), Craig Dugan (6, 9), Steve Hall (8)

Patriot High School

Client: Jurupa Unified School District
Design Principal: Nick Seierup
Managing Principal: Robert Lavey
Project Manager: Sandra Corrazelli
Senior Designer: Marcelo Igonda
Project Architect: Seth Sakamoto
Project Team: Jeffrey Capistran, Leigh Christy
Image Credits: Fred Daly (1–2, 4, 6), Conrado Lopez (5)

Perspectives Charter School

Client: Perspectives Charter School
Design Principal: Ralph E. Johnson
Managing Principal: Steve Turckes
Project Managers: Eric Spielman, Crandon Gustafson
Project Designer: Rusty Walker
Project Architect: Jim Skalla
Project Team: Pat Grzybek, Eric Kuntz, Ellen Mills, Vijay Patel, Thomas Smith
Image Credits: James Steinkamp (1–4, 7–8)

Peter O. Kohler Pavilion

Client: Oregon Health & Science University
Associate Architects: Petersen Kolberg & Associates
Design Principal: Nick Seierup
Managing Principal: Eric Van Aukee
Planning Principal: Jean Mah
Project Managers: Randy Larsen, Bob Cull
Senior Project Designer: Stan Chiu
Project Architect: Paul Kelsey
Project Team: Sing-Sing Lee, Jim Meyerhoff, Takeshi Namba, Bill Nation, Cesar Pineda, Ebi Saberi, Marilyn Smith, James Stafford, Thomas Ta
Image Credits: Rick Keating (1), Peter Eckert (2, 3)

Research Triangle Park Office of Perkins+Will

Client: Perkins+Will
Managing Principals: David Brownlee, Joseph R. Wagner
Design and Project Architect: Steve Hall
Interior Project Designers: Susan Lee, Laura Lada
Project Team: Katelyn Baird, Scott Lagstrom, Mark Paskanik,
  Rodrigo Reyes
Image Credits: Mark Herboth (1–2, 5–8)

Richard E. Lindner Center
George & Helen Smith Athletics Museum

Client: University of Cincinnati
Design Principal: Eva L. Maddox
Account Manager: Brian Weatherford
Project Team: Patrick Grzybek, Sheila Picchione, Becky Ruehl-Amann,
  Ron Stelmarski, Malgorzata Zawislak
Image Credits: Steve Hall for Hedrich Blessing (1–5)

Saint Cloud Technical College (SCTC) Workforce Center
Addition & Renovation

Client: Minnesota State Colleges & Universities System (MNSCU)
Design Principal: David Dimond
Project Manager: Laurence Page
Senior Designer: Paul Neuhaus
Project Architect: Doug Pierce
Project Team: Trevor Dickie, Sara Guyette, David Koenen, Linda Landry,
  Beth Latto, Tony Layne, Todd Lenthe, Jen Somers, Jeff Ziebarth,
  Phil Zittel
Image Credits: Peter Kerze (1, 3–4, 8), Lucie Marusin (2, 5, 7)

Sanford-Burnham Medical Research Institute at Lake Nona

Client: Tavistock Group
Design Principal: Pat Bosch
Managing Principal and Research Planner: Gary Shaw
Project Manager: Dana Anderson
Senior Designers: John McDonald, Camila Querasian and Angel Suarez
Project Architects: Jose Bofill, Sindu Meier
Project Team: Myoung Joo Chun, Hisham Elgadi, Maryam Katouzian,
  Jean Kim, Yong Lee, Lincoln Linder, Fiona Santos, Leslie Sims
Image Credits: New York Focus (1, 5)

Signature Place

Client: Cantor Development
Consulting Architect: Timothy Clemmons, Clemmons Architecture
Design Principal: Ralph E. Johnson
Managing Principal: Jose Gelabert-Navia
Project Managers: Yovanna Alvarez, Carlos Chiu
Project Designer: Cengiz Yetken
Project Architect: Hans Thummel
Project Team: Gustavo Alfonso, Brett Appel, Dan Biver, Jose Bofill,
  Yong Cai, Denise Gonzalez, Carrie Hunziker, Marlene Liriano,
  Bryan Schabel
Image Credits: James Steinkamp (1–5)

Skybridge

Client: Dearborn Development Company
Design Principal: Ralph E. Johnson
Managing Principals: G. William Doerge, Terrance Owens
Technical Principal: Fred Afshari
Project Designer: Curt Behnke
Project Architect: Ken Soch
Project Team: Jack Bransfield, Raymond Coleman, Malaika Corsentino,
  Aimee Eckmann, Brian Junge, Monica Oller, Rick Reindel,
  Bryan Schabel, Jim Skalla
Image Credits: James Steinkamp (1–2, 4, 6), Nick Merrick for Hedrich
  Blessing (3, 7)

TELUS House

Client: TELUS Corporation
Design Principals: Peter Busby, Jim Huffman
Project Manager: Jim Huffman
Project Team: Randy Bens, Brian Billingsley, David Dove, Robert Drew, Scott Edwards, Mike Elkan, Robin Glover, Mike Johnston, Marco Bonaventura, Ben Duffell, Mike McColl, Teryl Mullock, Deborah Nielsen, Martin Nielsen, Susan Ockwell, Steve Palmier, Richard Peck, Drahan Petrovic, Jenna South, Brian Wakelin, Alfred Waugh, Brent Welty, Terry Winkler
Designlines Ltd: S. Khattak, Soren Schou
Image Credits: Martin Tessler (1–7)

The Clare at Water Tower

Client: Franciscan Sisters of Chicago Service Corporation
Design Principal: Ralph Johnson
Managing Principals: Bridget Lesniak, Paul Donalson
Project Designer: Thomas Demetrion
Project Architect: Robert Neper
Project Team: Karla Brand, Bryce De Reynier, Gordon Gilmore, Tara Rejniak, Rick Young
Image Credits: James Steinkamp (1–3, 5–6)

The Silver Sea

Client: Concord Pacific Group
Design Principals: Peter Busby, Jim Huffman
Managing Principal: Jim Huffman
Project Team: Omer Arbel, Matt Galloway, Veronica Gillies, Sergio Jaramillo, Vahid Massah
Image Credits: Enrico Dagostini (2–6)

The Watermark

Client: Tuscan Development
Design Principal: Jim Merriman
Managing Principal: Jim Merriman
Senior Designer: Rick Kazebee
Project Designer: Rick Kazebee
Project Team: Anton Pretorius
Image Credits: Cameron Triggs (1–3, 5–6)

University of Washington School of Medicine Phase 2

Client: University of Washington
Managing Principal: Anthony Gianopoulos
Planning Principal: Tully Shelley
Project Manager: Anthony Gianopoulos
Project Designer: Andrew Clinch
Project Architect: Andrew Clinch
Project Team: Sara Robinson, Kelly Schnell
Image Credits: Benjamin Benschneider (1–4, 6–9)

Wallis Annenberg Research Center

Client: House Ear Institute
Design Principals: Nick Seierup, James Stafford
Managing Principal: Eric Van Aukee
Lab Planning Principal: Gary Shaw
Project Manager: Boon Lim
Project Architect: Cindy O'Bleness
Technical Coordinator: Scott Allen
Image Credits: Benny Chan/Fotoworks (1–5)

ON THE BOARDS

Al-Birr Foundation Office Tower

Client: Al-Birr Foundation
Design Principal: Rob Goodwin
Project Team: Jason Allen, Joaquin Bonifaz, Serge Khoudessian,
    Erik G. L'Heureux
Image Credits: Perkins+Will

Atlanta BeltLine Corridor Design

Client: Atlanta BeltLine, Inc.
Project Team: Heather Alhadeff, Leo Alvarez, Kevin Bacon,
    Thomas Boeman, Geoff Boyd, Cassie Branum, Manuel Cadrecha,
    Ryan Gravel, David Green, Tom Grimwood, Paul Knight,
    Kimberly Lindstrom, Eva L. Maddox, Martin Nielsen, Nat Slaughter,
    Chad Stacy, Eric Stedman, Pamela Steiner, Alexander Stewart,
    Li Sun, John Threadgill, Jeffrey Williams
Image Credits: Perkins+Will

Beirut Hotel and Residences

Client: Confidential
Design Principal: R. Anthony Fieldman
Managing Principal: Imad Ghantous
Project Manager: Hassan Gardezi
Senior Designers: Marc el-Khouri, Yong Huang
Project Team: Alan Ho, Scott Kirkham, Cristina Zancani
Image Credits: Perkins+Will

Calexico West Border Station

Client: General Services Administration (GSA)
Design Principal: Allison Williams
Managing Principal/Project Manager: Marc Arnold
Senior Designer: Aaron Harcek
Project Interior Designer: David Charette
Project Architect: Robert Clocker
Technical Coordinators: Nilda Marchan, Mayank Singh
Project Team: Kasper Bigosinski, Tom Boeman, Erinn Dornaus,
    Ben Feldman, Rosannah Harding, Tyrone Marshall, Kristin Mjolsnes,
    Gretchen Mokry, Jaepyo Park, Pamela Paul, Steven Sanchez,
    Lynsey Schwab, Ram Subramanian
Image Credits: Gerald Ratto (1), Perkins+Will (2)

Campus for Research Excellence And Technological Enterprise

Client: National Research Foundation
Associate Architect: DP Architects, Singapore
Design Principal: Allison Williams
Managing Principal: Russ Drinker
Lab Planning Principal: Tully Shelly
Consulting Principals: Peter Busby, Dan Watch
Project Manager: Lynn Olechnowicz
Senior Designer: Scott Williams
Project Architects: Christine Chin, Haji Ishikawa
Project Team: Aimee Chan, Drake Hawthorne, Philip Luo,
    Tyrone Marshall, Kristin Mjolsnes, Jaepyo Park, Hyuek Rhee,
    Steven Sanchez, Ram Subramanian
Image Credits: Perkins+Will

College of Arts at Sabah Al-Salem University City–Kuwait University

Client: Sabah Al-Salem University
Associate Architect: Dar Al-Handasah
Design Principals: R. Anthony Fieldman, Joan Blumenfeld
Managing Principal: Michael Kihn
Project Manager: Edward Stand
Senior Designer: Michael Bardin
Project Designer: Kelly Powell
Project Architect: Adam Meredith
Project Team: Hye Yeon Cho, Steven Danielpour, Scott Finkler,
   Lindsey Homer, Kamalrukh Katrak, Justin Roznowski,
   Delkash Shaharian, Craig Sobeski
Image Credits: Perkins+Will

College of Education at Sabah Al-Salem University City–Kuwait University

Client: Sabah Al-Salem University
Associate Architect: Dar Al-Handasah
Design Principals: R. Anthony Fieldman, Joan Blumenfeld
Managing Principal: Michael Kihn
Project Manager: Edward Stand
Senior Designer: Scott Kirkham
Project Designers: Dutch Osborne, Susana Takayama
Project Architect: Scott Yocom
Project Team: Steven Danielpour, Kamalrukh Katrak, Ming Leung,
   Katherine Lytle, Dennis Park, Arjav Shah, Calvin Smith,
   Junghee Sung, Minho Yang
Image Credits: Perkins+Will

CP-70 (High-Rise Competition)

Client: Confidential
Design Principals: David Hansen, William Hendrix
Managing Principal: Rusty Meadows
Project Manager: Amy Averill
Project Designers: Ron Stelmarski, Kevin Johnson, Shub Sanyal
Project Team: Peter Chmielewski, Hussein Cholkmany, Yuki Gottschaldt,
   Moez Jaffer, Regina Kinny, Chris Lee, Natascha Zizac
Image Credits: Perkins+Will

Dallas International School

Client: Dallas International School
Design Principal: Agus Rusli
Managing Principal: Patrick Glenn
Project Manager: Patrick Glenn
Project Designers: Gordon Gilmore, Ashwin Toney, Kevin Mereness
Project Architect: Liz Ann Cordill
Project Team: DJ Christgen
Image Credits: Perkins+Will

Desertcreat College

Client: Police Service of Northern Ireland
Design Principal: R. Anthony Fieldman
Managing Principal: Ray Clark
Project Manager: Taidg O'Malley
Senior Project Designers: Scott Kirkham, Michael Bardin
Project Architect: Sergio Neissen
Planning + Strategies: Janice Barnes, Sonya Dufner
Project Team: Matthew Downs, Mina Guirguis, Alison Kwiatkowski,
   Katherine Lytle, Minho Yang
Image Credits: Perkins+Will

Florida International University Academic Health Sciences Center

Client: Florida International University
Design Principals: Pat Bosch, Marlene Liriano
Managing Principal: Gene Kluesner
Project Manager: George Valcarcel
Project Team: Yenny Calabrese, Lilia Gonzalez, John Hoffman, Yong Lee, Damian Ponton, Angel Suarez
Image Credits: Perkins+Will

Heping Residential Development

Client: Tianjin Tianchuang Real Estate Co., Ltd.
Associate Architect: Tianjin Real Estate Appraise Survey & Design Institute
Design Principal: Ralph E. Johnson
Managing Principal: G. William Doerge
Project Manager: Heather Poell
Project Designers: Curt Behnke, Yong Cai
Project Architects: Ken Soch, JB Park
Project Team: Daniel Festag, Jason Flores, Nathan Freise, Phillip Hung, Kyle Knudson, Rusty Walker, Cengiz Yetken
Image Credits: Perkins+Will

Kempinski Hotel and Residences SailTower

Client: Al-Issa Real Estate Development Company
Associate Architect: Mohamed Harasani Architects
Design Principal: Robert Goodwin
Managing Principal: Imad Ghantous
Project Manager: Hassan A. Gardezi
Senior Designer: Erik L'Heureux
Project Architects: Reza Bostani, Joaquin Bonifaz
Project Team: Eva Leung
Image Credits: Perkins+Will

LA Courthouse

Client: General Services Administration (GSA)
Design Principals Ralph E. Johnson, Gary Wheeler
Managing Principal: Aki Knezevic
Technical Principal: Fred Afshari
Project Managers: Eric Spielman, Bridget Lesniak, Paul Clinch, Frank Pettinati
Project Designers: Thomas Mozina, Thomas Demetrion
Project Architects: Marius Ronnett, Robert Neper
Project Team: Julian Barajas, Nicolette Brandstedt, Geoffrey Brooksher, Yong Cai, Kimberly Creswell, Bryce de Renier, Yan Ding, Colin Drake, Jeffrey Frank, Roberto Gonzalez, Jason Hall, Hahn Joh, Chinatsu Kaneko, Tamara Kent, Jay Lane, June Oh, Monica Oller, Avni Patel, Vijay Patel, Guillame Petit, Michael Rafferty, Kristin Roseborough, Jason Rosenblatt, William Schmalz, Laura Smith, Lindsay Steinacher, Heekyung Sung, Khai Toh, Rusty Walker, Mariah Walters, Zhenyu Wang, Cengiz Yetken, Austin Zike
Image Credits: Perkins+Will (1, 3–4), James Steinkamp (2)

Merchant Square

Client: European Land and Properties
Design Principal: Ralph E. Johnson
Managing Principal: Raymond Clark
Technical Principal: Bruce Toman
Project Director: Taidg O'Malley
Project Manager: Jon Gibson
Project Designer: Todd Snapp
Project Architects: Ian Bush, Jane Cameron, Kamalrukh Katrak, Hans Thummel
Project Team: Brett Appel, Susan Barr, Curt Behnke, Yong Cai, Man Chun Chan, Tom Demetrion, Daniel Festag, Emma Foster, Adam Freise, Yuki Gottschaldt, Jeff Hayner, John Kitson, Chris Lee, Michael McPhail, Nicholas Michelin, Jerico Prater, Michael Rafferty, Bryan Schabel, Mariah Walters
Image Credits: Perkins+Will

Musée de Louvain-la-Neuve

Client: Louvain-la-Neuve
Associate Architect: Bureau D'Architecture, Emile Verhaegen
Design Principal: Ralph E. Johnson
Managing Principal: Aki Knezevic
Project Designer: Todd Snapp
Project Team: Abul Abdullah, Dana Arnold, Yuki Gottschaldt, Jeff Hayner,
    Nicholas Michelin, Tara Rejniak, Chris Weatherford, Nick Wilson
Image Credits: Perkins+Will

Oklahoma Medical Research Foundation Research Tower

Client: Oklahoma Medical Research Foundation
Design Principal: Manuel Cadrecha
Managing Principal: Dan Watch
Project Manager: Mark Rahe
Project Designer: David Rogers
Interior Designer: Grace Paul
Project Team: Leehong Chen, Andrew Chrenshaw, Yves Gauthier,
    Steffi Kuehnlein, Scott Maddux, Scott Sandlin, Andres Stell,
    Jonathan Stokes
Image Credits: Perkins+Will

Oriental Fisherman's Wharf

Client: Shanghai Oriental Fisherman's Wharf Development Company
Associate Architect: Shanghai institute of Architectural Design &
    Research Co. Ltd.
Design Principal: Ralph E. Johnson
Managing Principal: G. William Doerge
Project Managers: William Berger, Xinfang Chen
Project Architect: Marius Ronnett
Project Designer: Carl Knutson
Project Team: Max Adams, Jason Flores, Jenny Hu, Brad Lightner,
    Li Pan, Bryan Schabel, Joe Wang, Cenzig Yetken
Image Credits: Perkins+Will

Rush University Medical Center, Campus Transformation Project

Client: Rush University Medical Center
Design Principals: Ralph Johnson, Jerry Johnson
Managing Principal: James Zajac
Planning Principals: Jocelyn Frederick, Jean Mah
Technical Principal: Bruce Toman
Project Directors: Walter Bissonnette, Bridget Lesniak
Project Managers: Denis O'Malley, Paul Clinch, Eric Spielman
Senior Design Architects: John Moorhead, Tom Demetrion, Jose Valeros
Senior Interior Designers: Jason Rosenblatt, Rod Vickroy,
    Barbara Burnette
Senior Technical Architects: James Nowak, Jack Lesniak, Mark Walsh,
    Patrick Gryzbek
Senior Interior Architect: Robert Cohoon
Senior Medical Planners: Brent Hussong, Laura Zimmer, Zahra Makki,
    Bill Nation, Patricia Canedo
Project Designer: Jeff Saad
Project Architects: David Archer, Carlos Barillas, Milan Miladinovich,
    JB Park, Justin Aleo, Nathan Fell
Medical Planner: Marvina Williams
Interior Design Technical Coordinator: Michael Tucker
Project Team: Max Adams, Leigh Allen, Gelacio Arias, Joseph Barnes,
    Scott Blindauer, Matt Booma, Andrew Broderick, Crister Cantrell,
    Bernard Chung, Derya Civelekoglu, Rebecca Cox, Reginald Dorce,
    Daniel Ferrario, Latricia Gordon, Michelle Halle Stern, Joel Jacobson,
    Hannah Jefferies, Remiko Kitazawa, Michelle Malecha, Aaron Manns,
    Michael Margulis, Jennifer Merchant, Saul Moreno, Hugo Prill,
    Christina Sapienza, Joachim Schuessler, Aashit Shah, Paul Stovesand,
    Young Sup Park, Amy Swift, Sawat Tulyathorn
Image Credits: Perkins+Will

Saadiat Marina SM5-11

Client: ACTG Development
Design Principal: William Hendrix
Managing Principal: William Hendrix
Project Manager: Amy Averill
Senior Designer: Kevin Johnson
Project Designers: Moez Jaffer, Kent McCullough
Project Team: Eunjoo Cho, Hari Rangarajan
Image Credits: Perkins+Will

Shanghai Eastern Hepatobiliary Hospital

Client: Shanghai Eastern Hepatobiliary Hospital
Design Principal: Ralph E. Johnson
Managing Principal: G. William Doerge
Project Manager: Xinfang Chen
Project Designer: Todd Snapp
Project Team: Todd Accardi, Evan Cai, Chooyan Han, Kyle Knudson,
   Neil McCallum, Li Pan, Joe Wang, Justin Woo, Laura Zimmer
Image Credits: Perkins+Will

Shanghai High School International Division

Client: Shanghai High School
Design Principal: Ralph E. Johnson
Managing Principals: Chris Reynolds, Steve Turckes
Project Manager: Xinfang Chen
Project Designer: Jeff Saad
Project Team: Daniel Ferrario, Aaron Manns, Joe Wang, Justin Woo,
   Lorraine Zhang
Image Credits: Perkins+Will

Shanghai Nature Museum

Client: Shanghai Science & Technology Museum
Associate Architect: Architectural Design & Research Institute of
   Tongji University Co., Ltd.
Design Principal: Ralph E. Johnson
Managing Principal: G. William Doerge
Project Manager: Xinfang Chen
Project Designers: Bryan Schabel, Thomas Demetrion
Project Architect: Marius Ronnett
Project Team: Abul Abdullah, Matt Booma, Xichun Cai, Yi Cai, Yong Cai,
   Daniel Ferrario, Daniel Festag, Adam Freise, Nathan Freise,
   Chengyan Hu, Yun Hua, Leila Kanar, Kyle Knudson, Nicholas Michelin,
   Li Pan, Todd Snapp, Michael Tumminello, Jun Wang, Yune Xie
Image Credits: Perkins+Will

Spaulding Rehabilitation Hospital

Client: Spaulding Rehabilitation Hospital
Design Principal: Ralph E. Johnson
Managing Principal: Tim Marsters
Project Designer:Mike McPhail
Senior Technical: Robert Neper
Project Managers: Paul Clinch; Jessica Stebbins
Project Architects: Bryce Tolene; Mike Heath
Project Team: Max Adams, Juliette Bowker, Allen Buie, Blaine
   Campbell, Christopher Karlson, Erin Keegan, Jeffrey Keilman,
   Michelle Malecha, Shane Mathewson, Joanell Mueller, Deborah
   Rivers, Dan Stubbs
Image Credits: Perkins+Will

Tianjin Museum

Client: Tianjin Design Service Co. Ltd. for Construction Project
Associate Architect: HH Design
Design Principal: Ralph E. Johnson
Managing Principal: G. William Doerge
Project Manager: Xinfang Chen
Project Designer: Todd Snapp
Project Team: Chooyon Han, Jenny Hu, Kyle Knudson, Nicholas Michelin
Image Credits: Perkins+Will

Universidade Agostinho Neto

Client: Ministry of Education and Culture
Design Principal: Ralph E. Johnson
Managing Principal: G. William Doerge
Project Managers: Walt Heffernan, Dave Gutierrez
Project Designers: Thomas Demetrion, Cengiz Yetken
Project Architects: Ken Soch, Marius Ronnett
Project Team: Todd Accardi, Nathalie Belanger, Walter Bissonnette,
  Nicolette Brandstedt, Kathlene Bruner, Yong Cai, David Carr,
  Deborah Chase, Raymond Coleman, Kimberly Cook, Kimberly Creswell,
  Lori Day, Flavia de Almeida, Bryce de Renier, Jeffrey Frank,
  Molly Frascogna, Mark Hartmann, Jeff Hayner, Brantley Hightower,
  Chinatsu Kaneko, Kyle Knudson, Michael McPhail, Gokul Natarajan,
  Angel Ortiz, Vijay Patel, Paula Pilolla, John Ruthven,
  Stephen Scharlach, Karen Schuman, Gavin Smith, Thomas Smith,
  Todd Snapp, Linda Swain, Rusty Walker, Mark Walsh, Zhenyu Wang,
  Michael Weiner, Austin Zike
Image Credits: Perkins+Will

Xi'an Jiaotong Liverpool University Integrated Science Building

Client: Xi'an Jiaotong Liverpool University
Design Principal: Robert Goodwin
Project Manager: John Wright
Project Designer: Michael Bardin
Project Architects: Xinfang Chen, Anthony Alfieri
Project Team: Ahmad Bostani, Sally Hinderegger, Jenny Hu, Ye Rin Kin,
  Pan Li, Sergio Neissen, Cheryl Woo
Image Credits: Perkins+Will

Awards List

LEGACY

100 North Riverside

1993 National Honor Award–Office Building, AIA
1992 Distinguished Building Award, AIA, Chicago Chapter
1991 Certificate of Merit–Interior Architecture, AIA, Chicago Chapter

Crate & Barrel Corporate Headquarters

2003 Distinguished Building Award, AIA, Chicago Chapter

McDonnell Pediatric and Cancer Research Building

2001 Distinguished Building Award, AIA, Chicago Chapter
2001 Distinguished Building Award, AIA, St. Louis Chapter

Neuroscience Research Building

2005 Distinguished Building Award, AIA, Chicago Chapter
2004 Citation Award, AIA, Los Angeles Chapter

Orland Park Village Center

1990 Distinguished Building Award, AIA, Chicago Chapter

Peggy Notebaert Nature Museum

2000 American Architecture Award, The Chicago Athenaeum
2000 Distinguished Building Award, AIA, Chicago Chapter

Perry Community Educational Village

1996 National Honor Award–School K12, AIA
1995 Distinguished Building Award, AIA, Chicago Chapter
1994 Crow Island School Citation, *American School & University*
1993 Honor Award, AIA, Cleveland Chapter
1993 The Shirley Cooper Award, American Association of School
       Administrators and the AIA

Temple Hoyne Buell Hall

1998 Distinguished Building Award, AIA, Chicago Chapter
1998 Interior Architecture Honor Award, AIA, Chicago Chapter

Terminal 5, O'Hare International Airport

1993 Distinguished Building Award, AIA, Chicago Chapter
1993 Divine Detail Award, AIA, Chicago Chapter
1993 Interior Architecture Award, AIA, Chicago Chapter

Tribune Interactive

2003 Divine Detail Honorable Mention, AIA, Chicago Chapter
2002 Interior Architecture National Honor Award, AIA
2002 Distinguished Building Award, AIA, Chicago Chapter
2002 Interior Architecture Award, AIA, Chicago Chapter

Troy High School

1994 National Honor Award, AIA
1993 Distinguished Building Award, AIA, Chicago Chapter
1993 Architectural Citation, *American School & University*

CURRENT

Arizona State University, Interdisciplinary Science & Technology Building I

2010 Architectural Commendation Award, Perkins+Will Biennale
2009 Distinguished Building Award, AIA, Chicago Chapter
2007 Sustainability Award, AIA, Chicago Chapter
2007 Energy Award, AIA, Arizona Chapter
2007 Merit Award, AIA, California Chapter
2007 Merit Award, AIA, Arizona Chapter
2007 Sustainable Resource Planning Award, AIA, Arizona Chapter
2006 Outstanding Building Award, *American School & University*
2004 Design Excellence/Work in Progress Recognition, *American School & University*

Atrisco Heritage Academy

2009 Grand Prize National School Boards Association, Exhibition of School Architecture
2009 Design Concept Award, School Planning and Architectural Exhibition Awards, Council of Educational Facility Planners
2009 Citation for Design Award, AIA, Pasadena & Foothill Chapter
2008 Design Award, AIA, San Fernando Valley Chapter

August Wilson Center for African American Culture

2008 Merit Award, National Organization of Minority Architects

Bank of America Corporate Center (Workplace Prototype)

2008 Honorable Mention, Contract–Offices over 10,000 SF, ASID, Illinois Chapter

Blythewood High School

2007 Honor Award, AIA, South Carolina Chapter
2007 Educational Facility Design Awards, AIA Committee on Architecture for Education
2006 Merit Award, AIA, Columbia Chapter

Brentwood Town Center Station

2004 Medal for Excellence, Lieutenant Governor of BC
2004 Medal for Excellence, Governor General of Canada
2004 AIA 8th Annual Business Week/Architectural Record Awards, Finalist
2003 Consulting Engineers of BC, Award of Excellence in Building Engineering
2003 Structural Achievement Commendation, UK Institute of Structural Engineers
2003 Award of Excellence, UK Institute of Structural Engineers
2003 Consulting Engineers of BC Section Award, Illuminating Engineering Society of North America, IIDA and Vision Awards
2002 CISC Awards for Excellence, Honourable Mention for an Outstanding Steel Structure
2000 Bentley Success Award, Transportation Design and Engineering

CDC National Center for Environmental Health Building 110

2006 Best of the Best Award for Green Building, IIDA, Georgia Chapter
2006 CDC Division of Laboratory Sciences, Partners in Public Health Improvement

Center for Urban Waters

2008 Regional Top Ten Award, AIA, Seattle Chapter
2008 Civic Design Merit Award, AIA, Washington Chapter

Chervon International Trading Company

2010 Architectural Design Award, Perkins+Will Biennale
2009 Mies van der Rohe Citation of Merit Award, AIA, Illinois Chapter
2008 Distinguished Building Award, AIA, Chicago Chapter

Computer Sciences Building

2004 Natural Resources Canada, Energy Efficiency Award
(Honourable Mention)
2002 Association of Canadian Consulting Engineers, Canadian
Consulting Engineering Awards, Award of Excellence, 2nd Place
2002 International Green Building Award, World Architecture
2002 Medal of Excellence, Governor General of Canada
2002 Medal of Excellence, Lieutenant Governor of BC
2000 International Green Building Challenge

Confidential Financial Services Client

2007 First Place Award, Contract–Over 10,000 SF, ASID, Illinois
Chapter
2007 Best New Briefing Center in the World, Association of Briefing
Program Managers

Contemporaine

2010 Architectural Design Award, Perkins+Will Biennale
2006 Multifamily Housing Award, AIA
2005 National Honor Award for Architecture, AIA
2005 Distinguished Building Award, AIA, Chicago Chapter

Darden Restaurants Corporate Headquarters Building

2010 Award of Excellence, Built Category, AIA, Orlando Chapter
2010 Best of the Best Forum Design Awards–Corporate Category,
IIDA, Georgia Chapter

Dockside Green

2008 GLOBE Awards for Environmental Excellence, Excellence in
Urban Sustainability
2007 BC Hydro Power Smart Excellence Award Winner, Innovation in
Sustainable Building Design
2006 Smart Growth BC, Process/Proposal Award
2006 Merit Award–Approved or Adopted Urban Design Plan, Urban
Design Awards, Royal Architectural Institute of Canada
2005 Award of Excellence, Canadian Architect
2005 Brownie Award, Best Overall Project, Canadian Urban Institute
2005 Brownie Award, Green Design and Technology, Canadian Urban
Institute
2005 Planning Institute of BC, Innovation in Site Planning and
Design Award

Equal Employment Opportunity Commission (EEOC)

2009 Honor Award, AIA, Virginia Chapter
2009 Bronze Award, IIDA, Mid-Atlantic Chapter

Great River Energy Headquarters

2010 Sustainable Design FAB Award, IIDA, Northland Chapter
2010 Member's Choice FAB Award, IIDA, Northland Chapter
2009 Honor Award, AIA, Minnesota Chapter
2009 Committee On The Environment Top Ten Award, AIA
2009 Merit Award, AIA, Minneapolis Chapter
2009 Design Award of Merit, Society of American Registered Architects
2008 Engineering Excellence Award, American Council of
Engineering Companies
2008 Honor Award, American Planning Association, Minnesota Chapter
2008 Governor's Award for Pollution Control
2008 Grand Award, American Council of Engineering Companies,
Minnesota Chapter

Haworth Showrooms

2010 Interior Design Award, Perkins+Will Biennale
2009 Silver Award–Retail Design, Interior Designers Institute of British Columbia
2008 Environmental Design Category, Big "I" International Interior Awards, *Contract* Magazine
2008 First Place Award–Retail Design, ASID, Illinois Chapter
2008 Honorable Mention, Contract–Retail, ASID, Illinois Chapter
2008 NeoCon Best Large Showroom Award, IIDA
2007 Interior Architecture Institute of Honor Award, AIA
2007 Gold Award–Retail, IIDA, Mid-Atlantic Chapter
2007 Special Merit Award–Sustainability, IIDA, Mid-Atlantic Chapter
2007 First Place Award–Green Design, ASID, Illinois Chapter
2006 First Place–Retail Design, ASID, Illinois Chapter
2006 Interior Architecture Award Citation of Merit, AIA, Chicago Chapter
2005 Interior Design Award, Best of Competition, IIDA
2004 Green Design Award, ASID
2004 Best Large Showroom Award, IIDA
2004 NeoCon Best in Show, IIDA

Hector P. Garcia Middle School

2008 Award of Excellence and Design–Best of K12, *Texas Construction*
2008 Excellence in Design–Honorable Mention, *Environmental Design + Construction*
2008 Educational Appropriateness Award, Texas Association of School Administrators and School Boards
2008 Sustainability Award, Texas Association of School Administrators and School Boards
2008 Outstanding Educational Award, Association of General Contractors America
2008 Summit Award, Association of General Contractors America
2007 Merit Award, AIA, Dallas Chapter
2006 Studio Design Award, Texas Society of Architects

Intrepid Sea, Air & Space Museum

2010 Interiors Commendation Award, Perkins+Will Biennale
2009 Honorable Mention–Institutional Category, ASID, Illinois Chapter
2009 Interior Architecture Citation of Merit, AIA, Chicago Chapter

INVISTA Inc., Antron®
DuPont Antron® Resource Center

2005 Best Showroom/Exhibit, *Contract* Magazine Big "I" International Interior Awards
2005 First Place Award, Retail Category, ASID, Illinois Chapter
2005 Outstanding Achievement Award, HOW International Design Competition
2005 Signage & Environmental Graphics Category, American Corporate Identity Annual
2005 Signage & Environmental Graphics Category, Creativity Design Annual
2004 Interior Design Award, Best of Competition, IIDA
2004 Signage & Environmental Graphics Category, Creativity Design Annual
2004 Interior Architecture Honor Award, AIA, Chicago Chapter
2004 Award of Excellence, Environmental Graphics Category, Communication Arts Design Annual
2003 Certificate of Design Excellence, Print International Business Graphics Competition
1991 Best Showroom Renovation/Best of West Week, ASID
1991 Best Exhibition Design/Best of West Week, ASID
1991 Best Retail Environment/Best of West Week, ASID
1991 Honor Award, NeoCon Product Display Competition, AIA

Labovitz School of Business and Economics

2010 Architectural Design Award, Perkins+Will Biennale

Los Angeles Police Department Rampart Station

2010 Certificate of Merit, AIA, Academy of Architecture for Justice
2009 "Green Building of the Year" Award, Architectural Award of Excellence, Los Angeles Architectural Awards, Los Angeles Business Council
2009 Merit Award, Sustainable Category, Concrete Masonry Association of California and Nevada/AIACC
2009 Westside Prize, Westside Urban Forum
2008 American Public Works Association Award
2008 Community Impact Award (City of LA Green Building Program), Los Angeles Architectural Awards, Los Angeles Business Council
2006 Award of Merit, AIA, Academy of Architecture for Justice
2005 Citation Award, AIA, San Fernando Valley Chapter
2004 Architectural Excellence Award, City of LA Cultural Affairs Commission

Materials Testing Laboratory

2001 AIBC Innovation Award
2001 International Design Resource Award, Honorable Mention
2000 Consulting Engineers of BC, Award of Merit
2000 What Makes it Green? AIA

Mayo Clinic Replacement Hospital

2009 Honor Award, AIA, Orlando Chapter

Miami Beach City Hall Annex

2006 Unbuilt Merit Award, AIA, Florida Chapter
2005 Design Award of Merit, Society of American Registered Architects
2005 Unbuilt Design Award Finalist, AIA, Miami Chapter

Nicola Valley Institute of Technology

2005 Canadian Wood Council, Wood Works High Performance Building Award
2005 Excellence in Architecture Award, AIA Committee on Education & Society for College and University Planning
2004 Medal for Excellence, Governor General of Canada
2002 Vancouver Regional Construction Association Awards of Excellence, General Contractors Award of Merit
2002 Wood Design Awards, Citation Award
2002 Medal for Excellence, Lieutenant Governor of BC
2001 What Makes it Green? AIA

Normand Maurice Building

2005 Canadian Institute of Steel Construction (CISC), BC Region Steel Design Award of Excellence, Architectural Category

North Campus Residence Hall

2010 Architectural Commendation Award, Perkins+Will Biennale
2010 Design Award, AIA, New England Chapter
2010 Honor Award for Design Excellence, Boston Society of Architects/AIA
2010 Merit Award for Excellence in Architecture, New Building, SCUP/AIA-CAE Excellence Awards
2010 Gold Award, *Building Design + Construction*, 13th Annual Building Team Awards

NYU Stern School of Business Concourse Renovation Project

2010 *American School & University* Magazine, Collegiate Citation for Higher Education
2010 Second Place–Educational/Institutional Category, IIDA Lester Dundes Award

Ohlone College Newark Center for Health Sciences and Technology

2009 Sustainable Built Environmental Award, Acterra
2009 Project Team Award, Platinum, *Building Design + Construction*
2008 Design Award of Merit, Community College Facility Coalition
2008 Environmental Hero Award, US Environment Protection Agency
2008 Green Achievement–Facilities Award, Green California Community College Summit
2008 Best Green Building Award, *California Construction*

One Haworth Center

2010 Architectural Commendation Award, Perkins+Will Biennale
2008 Good Design is Good Business Award, *BusinessWeek/ Architectural Record*

Patriot High School

2008 Leroy F. Greene Design Award, Coalition for Adequate School Housing and AIA California Chapter
2006 Merit Award for Sustainable Design, Concrete Masonry Association of California and Nevada
2006 Merit Award, AIA, Inland California Chapter
2005 Merit Award, AIA, Pasadena & Foothill Chapter
2005 Merit Award, AIA, Long Beach/South Bay Chapter
2001 Design Concept Award, Council of Educational Facility Planners International

Perspectives Charter School

2007 ULI Awards for Excellence Finalist, Urban Land Institute
2006 Merit Award, DesignShare
2006 Mies Van Der Rohe Award–Citation of Merit, AIA, Illinois Chapter
2006 Interior Architecture Award, AIA, Chicago Chapter
2005 Distinguished Building Award, AIA, Chicago Chapter

Peter O. Kohler Pavilion

2009 National Design Award, AIA American Academy of Architecture for Health
2009 Design Award, AIA, San Fernando Valley Chapter
2006 Honorable Mention–Modern Healthcare Design Award, AIA
2006 Honor Award–Institutional/Education, AIA, Pasadena & Foothill Chapter

Research Triangle Park Office of Perkins+Will

2009 Merit Award, AIA, North Carolina Chapter

Richard E. Lindner Center
George & Helen Smith Athletics Museum

2008 Sports/Entertainment Award, Big "I" International Interior Awards, *Contract* Magazine
2008 Interior Architecture Award, AIA, Chicago Chapter
2007 First Place Award–Institutional, ASID, Illinois Chapter

Saint Cloud Technical College (SCTC) Workforce Center Addition & Renovation

2008 Honor Award, AIA, Minnesota Chapter

Sanford-Burnham Medical Research Institute at Lake Nona

2010 Award of Merit for Sustainable Design, AIA, Orlando Chapter
2010 Award of Excellence, AIA, Orlando Chapter
2009 Excellence in Construction Eagle Award–Institution Associated Builders & Contractors

Skybridge

2004 National Honor Award, AIA
2003 Distinguished Building Award, AIA, Chicago Chapter

TELUS House

2009 Interior Design Institute of British Columbia Awards, Gold Award, Work Place Partial Category
2008 Medal for Excellence, Lieutenant Governor of BC
2008 Consulting Engineers of BC, Award of Excellence for Building Engineering
2008 Canadian Institute of Steel Construction (CISC), BC Region Steel Design Award of Excellence, Architectural Category
2002 *Canadian Glass* Magazine, Great Canadian Curtainwall Contest, First Place
2001 International Design Resource Award, First Place
2001 What Makes it Green? AIA
2000 National Energy Efficiency Award
2000 International Green Building Challenge
2000 Consulting Engineers of BC, Award of Excellence

The Watermark

2010 Architectural Commendation Award, Perkins+Will Biennale
2009 Design Award, AIA, North Carolina Chapter
2009 Design Award, AIA, Southeast Regional Chapter

University of Washington School of Medicine Phase 2

2009 Civic Design Honor Award, AIA, Washington Chapter

Wallis Annenberg Research Center

2010 Westside Prize, Westside Urban Forum
2008 Awards of Excellence, New Buildings Award–Commercial, Los Angeles Architectural Awards, Los Angeles Building Council
2006 Merit Award, AIA, Pasadena & Foothill Chapter
2005 Merit Award, AIA, Long Beach/South Bay Chapter
2005 Citation Award, AIA, San Fernando Valley Chapter
2005 Unbuilt Award of Excellence, Los Angeles Architectural Awards, Los Angeles Business Council

ON THE BOARDS

Al-Birr Foundation Office Tower

2010 Future Project Awards Winner–Tall Buildings, MIPIM/
       Architectural Review
2007 Unbuilt Merit Award, AIA, New York State Chapter

Calexico West Border Station

2010 Merit Award, AIA, San Francisco Chapter

College of Arts at Sabah Al-Salem University City–Kuwait University

2010 Award of Excellence, AIA, New York State Chapter
2009 Shortlist, Future Projects Award–Education Category, Unbuilt,
       World Architecture Festival

College of Education at Sabah Al-Salem University City–Kuwait University

2010 Education Sector Award, Unbuilt, World Architecture News
2010 Innovative Curtain Wall Design, Citation, AIA, New York Chapter
2010 Award of Merit, AIA, New York State Chapter

Heping Residential Development

2006 Urban Design Award, AIA, Chicago Chapter

Kempinski Hotel and Residences SailTower

2010 Unbuilt Commendation Award, Perkins+Will Biennale
2009 Future Project Awards Winner–Tall Buildings, MIPIM/
       Architectural Review
2009 Future Projects Award–Leisure Shortlist, Awards for Architecture
       in Emerging Markets

LA Courthouse

2003 Project Award, *Architectural Review* & MIPIM, Cannes, France

Shanghai Eastern Hepatobiliary Hospital

2010 Unbuilt Commendation Award, Perkins+Will Biennale

Universidade Agostinho Neto

2009 American Architecture Award, The Chicago Athenaeum
2009 8th International Biennale of Architecture and Urbanism,
       Honorable Mention, Brazilian Institute of Architects

Bibliography

Brubaker CW. *Planning and Designing Schools*. New York: McGraw-Hill, 1998.

Guenther R and Vittori G. *Sustainable Healthcare Architecture*. New Jersey: John Wiley & Sons, 2008.

Hansen DA. *Reshaping Corporate Culture*. Melbourne: The Images Publishing Group, 2005.

Johnson, R. *Buildings and Projects*. New York: Rizzoli International Publications, 1995.

Johnson, R. *Normative Modernism*. Italy: l'Arca Edizioni, 1998.

Master Architects Series V: Perkins & Will, Selected & Current Works. Melbourne: The Images Publishing Group, 2000.

Perkins LB and Cocking WD. *Schools*. Progressive Architecture Library. New York: Reinhold Publishing Corporation, 1949.

Perkins, Fellows and Hamilton. *Educational Buildings*. Chicago: Perkins, Fellows and Hamilton, 1925.

Perkins, LB. *Workplace for Learning*. New York: Reinhold Publishing Corporation, 1957.

Perkins+Will. *Ideas + Buildings: Collective Process*.

Perkins+Will. *Ideas + Buildings: Perspective*.

Suzuki D with contributing essays by Busby P, Wardle K, and Taggart J. *BUSBY: LEARNING SUSTAINABLE DESIGN*. Quebec and Vancouver: Janam Publications and Busby Perkins+Will Architects, 2007.

Watch D. *Building Type Basics for Research Laboratories*. New York: John Wiley & Sons, 2001.

Watch D. *Research for the Global Good: Supporting a Better World For All*. Melbourne: The Images Publishing Group, 2010.

Wheeler, ET. *Hospital Design and Function*. New York: McGraw Hill, 1964.

Wheeler, ET. *Hospital Modernization and Expansion*. New York: McGraw Hill, 1971.

Firm Profile

Perkins+Will collaborates with globally recognized clients to set worldwide standards for design innovation and service. The firm recognizes the knowledge and insights gained from its colorful history with every new endeavor. Lawrence B. Perkins and Philip Will, Jr.—college roommates at Cornell University—established the firm in 1935, quickly gaining national and international recognition for client service and design accomplishments in education and healthcare. Expansion was fast paced. The firm was soon garnering acclaim for its corporate + commercial + civic, higher education, and science + technology work. Perkins+Will established a stronghold in the Interiors discipline that reaches across all areas of the practice; Branded Environments, Planning + Strategies, and Urban Design expertise evolved in recent decades.

The firm was able to leverage its core competencies and global reputation and opened offices around the U.S., forging success stories across North America, Asia, Africa, the Middle East and Europe. Today, Perkins+Will has completed projects in multiple countries around the globe. It is privileged to be among the nation's most respected design firms with 75 years of award-winning work and the distinction of the American Institute of Architects (AIA) Firm of the Year Award and the 2010 National Building Museum Honor Award for Civic Innovation. Perkins+Will celebrates its rich history and continues to build a legacy that leads its clients into the future.

Sustainable, high-performance, and environmentally conscious design is the cornerstone of Perkins+Will's practice that informs every project. Among the staff—more than 1,500—are more LEED Accredited Professionals than any other design firm.

An international firm practicing regionally, Perkins+Will is always close to its clients. Expertise is shared across all offices. This inclusive strategy focuses on Perkins+Will's clients, communities, and vision, which have remained unchanged since the firm's founding 75 years ago—to craft *ideas + buildings that honor the broader goals of society.*

Firm Principals

Brian Aitken
Karen Alschuler
Leo Alvarez
Dana Anderson
Marc Arnold
D'Arcy Arthurs
David Asaud
Pat Askew
Eric Aukee
Duff Balmer
Janice Barnes
Anita Barnett
Carolyn BaRoss
Ray Beets
Bill Berger
Gina Berndt
Joan Blumenfeld
Chris Bormann
Holly Briggs
Meg Brown
Gabrielle Bullock
Ila Burdette
Peter Busby
Jim Bynum
Manuel Cadrecha
Phil Callison
Jeannine Campbell
Jo Carmen
Vance Cheatham
Ray Clark
David Collins
Joe Connell
Ed Cordes
Barbara Crum
Joe Dailey
Stevanie Demko
Coleman DeMoss

David Dimond
Bill Doerge
Paul Donaldson
David Dove
Russ Drinker
Tama Duffy Day
David Dymecki
Paul Eagle
Ed Feiner
Phil Fenech
R. Anthony Fieldman
Ben Fisher
Joyce Fownes
Andrew Frontini
John Fuller
Jose Gelabert-Navia
David Gieser
James Godfrey
Rob Goodwin
Robin Guenther
Susan Gushe
David Hansen
Phil Harrison
George Hellmuth
Richard Herring
Michael Hess
Rick Hintz
John Hogshead
Randy Hood
Dave Johnson
Jerry Johnson
Ralph Johnson
Mark Jolicoeur
Eileen Jones
Dennis Kaiser
Tom Kasznia
Mike Kihn

Aki Knezevic
Charles Knight
Kay Kornovich
Willard Lariscy
Randy Larsen
Robert Lavey
Bridget Lesniak
Jones Lindgren
Marlene Liriano
Mark Lutz
Eva L. Maddox
Jean Mah
Stephen Manlove
Tim Marsters
Blair McCarry
Gary McNay
James Merriman
Gary Miciunas
Richard Miller
Steve Miller
Steve Milner
Judy Mitchell
Daniel Moore
John Morris
Dave Mueller
Bill Nation
Martin Nielsen
Rich Nitzsche
Michael Palmer
Prakash Pinto
Steve Ploeger
Lisa Pool
Tom Reisenbichler
Ken Rohlfing
Ted Rozeboom
William Schmalz
Fred Schmidt

Nick Seierup
Murali Selvaraj
Gary Shaw
Tully Shelley
Amy Sickeler
Cathy Simon
Jimmy Smith
Sam Spata
Jeff Stebar
Brodie Stephens
Douglas Streeter
Bruce Toman
Steve Turckes
Jeffery Tyner
Andrea Vanecko
Wendell Vaughn
Bill Viehman
Dan Watch
Howard Weiss
Jeffrey Welter
Allison Williams
Gregory Williams
James Wood
Dede Woodring
Robert Young
James Zajac
Jeff Ziebarth

Office Locations

Atlanta
Boston
Charlotte
Chicago
Dallas
Dubai
Hartford
Houston
London
Los Angeles
Miami
Minneapolis
New York
Orlando
Philadelphia
Research Triangle Park
San Diego
San Francisco
Seattle
Shanghai
Toronto
Vancouver
Washington, DC

Index of Projects